Relentless

The Boston Globe

KCI SPORTS PUBLISHING

KCI Sports Publishing 3340 Whiting Avenue, Suite 5
Stevens Point, WI 54481
Phone: 1-800-697-3756 Fax: 715-344-2668
www.kcisports.com

ISBN: 978-1-940056-67-8 (paperback)
ISBN: 978-1-940056-66-1 (hardcover)
Printed in the United States of America

BOOK STAFF

EDITOR Janice Page
ASSISTANT EDITOR/WRITER Ron Driscoll
ART DIRECTOR Rena Anderson Sokolow
DESIGNER Cindy Babiain
RESEARCHERS/PROOFREADERS
Bobby Coleman, William Herzog, Jim Karaian,
Richard Kassirer, James Matte, Louis Sokolow,
Joe Sullivan, Lisa Tuite

PHOTOGRAPHERS

THE BOSTON GLOBE Yoon S. Byun: 73 (rally) ·
Barry Chin: 2, 18, 20, 51, 52, 53, 54, 55, 56, 76, 92,
93, 96, 118 (1) · Jim Davis: front cover, 6, 12, 14, 15,
19 (fan), 23, 25 (2), 27, 36 (2), 37 (top), 40, 41, 42,
46, 64, 66, 67, 68, 69 (4), 70, 74, 80, 81, 82, 85
(Ramirez), 100, 106, 109, 117, 118 (1), 125 (Martinez),
126, 128, back cover · Stan Grossfeld: 19 (9), 22,
24, 26, 28 (2), 29 (2), 37 (bottom), 39, 44, 72, 73,
104, 111, 113, 115 · Matthew J. Lee: 97, 118 (1) · Jessica
Rinaldi: 118 (1) · John Tlumacki: 5, 60, 91, 95, 119, 125
(Betts) · Frank O'Brien/Globe file photo (Boggs) 125.

ADDITIONAL PHOTOS COURTESY OF

Associated Press: Kathy Willens, 84 · Julie Jacobson,
85 (Devers) · Andrew Harnik, 88 · John Bazemore,
98 · AP File Photo/Ted Sande (Williams) 125. Getty
Images: 10 · Harry How, title page · Jeff Gross, 8 ·
Rob Carr, 13 · Kevork Djansezian, 19 (Kinsler) · Ezra
Shaw, 19 (Holt) · Tim Warner, 32 · Maddie Meyer, 45 ·
Bob Levey, 48, 49, 58 · Adam Glanzman, 102.

With special thanks to Boston Globe editor Brian
McGrory; Joe Sullivan, Matt Pepin, and the Boston
Globe sports department; Bill Greene and the Globe
photo department; Jane Bowman, Erin Maghran, and
Globe marketing; Peter Clark and the entire team at
KCI Sports Pubishing; Worzalla; Justin Brouckaert,
Todd Shuster, and Aevitas Creative Management.

In memoriam Lisa J. Sullo, designer, mentor, friend.

Front cover Mookie Betts, Andrew Benintendi, and
Steve Pearce celebrate their ALDS elimination of
the Yankees.

Back cover The Red Sox celebrate their ninth World
Series title and their fourth in 15 years.

CONTENTS

Principal owner John Henry has helped deliver four World Series titles in 16 years to those he considers the true owners of the Red Sox, the fans of New England.

To our fans,

The Boston Red Sox were not just the best team in baseball this year, they were one of the best baseball teams ever assembled.

That said, being the best doesn't always translate into a world championship — particularly in baseball. Teams can get hot at just the right time. Softly hit balls can fall in just the right places. Injuries can take a toll. The Red Sox have won four times in the last 15 years, making it seem like maybe it's not all that hard. It is.

The 2018 Boston Red Sox were all about character. Character in the way they approached the game, the way they enjoyed each other, and the way they appreciated their fans — the most committed and knowledgeable fans in baseball. The result was some of the best baseball we have ever seen in New England, played by one of the most memorable teams.

The record-breaking 108-win season wasn't enough. Come October, they had to beat a 100-win New York Yankees team that had hit a record number of home runs. After that came the 103-win Houston Astros, the defending world champions, one of the most complete clubs in history. And the Los Angeles Dodgers were a powerhouse — a team with a storied past and high expectations for the present.

Our success didn't happen by accident, but was built over time. We won the division the past two years. Almost all our best players were drafted through our farm system. On top of that, we went out and added Alex Cora and his amazing staff, and J.D. Martinez. These two guys represent two of the best investments the Red Sox have ever made.

Baseball history is replete with examples of highly-talented teams failing to translate their abilities into championships. What we couldn't possibly know in spring training is that there was simply no way this team was going to allow itself to be stopped. There are a lot of people we can credit with this fourth world championship, starting with Alex, Dave Dombrowski, Mookie Betts, J.D., Chris Sale, David Price, and Craig Kimbrel. But in baseball, over 162 regular season games and a month of postseason games, it takes an entire team supported by a larger organization. The relentlessness that you saw on the field was shared by countless members of our franchise off it.

Of course, there are the fans, who play a role that's larger than even the most diehard among you might imagine. The Red Sox are — more than any other baseball club — a reflection of your love for the game and your commitment to the cause, whether we finish first or last (as we've done now for seven consecutive years). You, like this 2018 club, never give up, and never stop pushing toward our ultimate goal — world championships. This club and its fans remain inseparable, indivisible, and Tom, Mike, Sam, and all of us within Fenway Sports Group and the Boston Red Sox organization appreciate how vital you are to our success. The players see it, hear it, and feel it every day and night at Fenway and beyond.

So thank you, Red Sox Nation! Please enjoy the magical memories contained in this book. I hope you will reflect warmly on this special season for years and even decades to come.

John

BY JOHN POWERS • Globe Staff

introduction

From the beginning there was the fear that it was just another tease, a spring and summer setup for an autumn debacle. The Red Sox won 17 of their first 19 games, ran away with the division title and set a franchise record with 108 victories. But for their supporters with lengthy memories the specters of 1946, 1967, 1975, 1978, 1986, and 2003 still floated above the Fens.

"We play in a city that sometimes winning is a relief," manager Alex Cora observed.

Yet along with the fear of failure across generations of fans, three championship banners in a decade's time also had elevated expectations to pinstriped levels. This year, the pennant was only a prelude. The Sox had to win it all — and so they did, with resilience and resolve.

"What a way to end it!" Cora proclaimed after Boston had squelched the Dodgers in five games to claim its first crown in five years while losing only three playoff outings. This one wasn't as cathartic as it was in 2004, as anticlimactic as in 2007 or as emotional as in 2013, but it was exceptionally satisfying. The best Boston bunch in 118 seasons was also the best at the end. "This is why I came to Boston," said pitcher David Price, who won two Series games, including the 5-1 finale, after hurling the pennant clincher against defending champion Houston.

With the exception of several crucial additions, most notably designated hitter J.D. Martinez, this was the same ballclub that had fallen short in 2017. The difference was the skipper, who'd played four seasons in Boston, earned a ring in 2007, and understood the delights and demands of playing here. "He's been through everything we're going through," said right fielder Mookie Betts. "He's done it. So there's no reason for us not to listen and to put what he says into action."

Cora's tranquil approach proved ideal for the rhythms and rigors of a 162-game grind plus a pressurized postseason. "He spoke about every day, turn the page, turn the page," said center fielder Jackie Bradley Jr. "Moving on to the next step, not dwelling on the past. What can we do for the present and what's going to help out for the future?"

Cora's composure and confidence in his crew were invaluable after the four-run home loss to New York in Game 2 of the ALDS. "The sky was falling in Boston," he said. "It seems like all of a sudden we weren't good."

His players responded with a 16-1 explosion in the Bronx, then closed out the Yankees, 4-3, with a photo-finish groundout that momentarily put their celebration on hold. Then, after taking a 7-2 home hammering from the Astros in the ALCS opener, the Sox finished off the series with three triumphs in Texas. "We don't shy away from adversity," declared pitcher Chris Sale, who came out of the bullpen to strike out the side in LA and sew up the Series. "We don't back down from a challenge."

The club's resilience was tested in Los Angeles when, on the night after losing Game 3 in 18 innings, Boston fell behind, 4-0, in the sixth and was facing a deadlocked series and the possibility of returning home for two elimination games. But Mitch Moreland's three-run pinch-hit homer in the seventh set off a nine-run outburst and put his mates in control. "One thing about our team, we keep playing," said Cora.

These Sox took the same approach in October that they did in April, performing with decidedly more grit than glamour. "We are a bunch of grinders," said Steve Pearce, the Series MVP who belted two homers in the clincher.

"The way we play day in and day out, we expect that of each other. This is exactly where we knew we were going to be." ◾

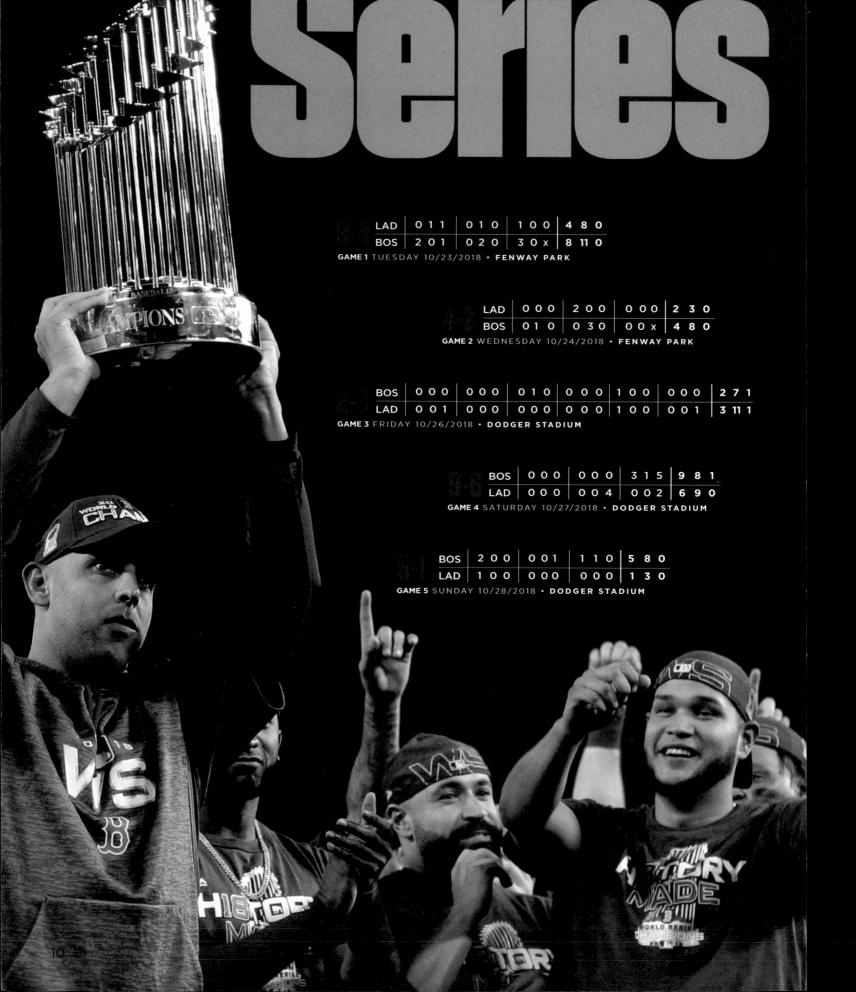

Series

LAD	0 1 1	0 1 0	1 0 0	4	8 0
BOS	2 0 1	0 2 0	3 0 x	8	11 0

GAME 1 TUESDAY 10/23/2018 • FENWAY PARK

LAD	0 0 0	2 0 0	0 0 0	2	3 0
BOS	0 1 0	0 3 0	0 0 x	4	8 0

GAME 2 WEDNESDAY 10/24/2018 • FENWAY PARK

BOS	0 0 0	0 0 0	0 1 0	0 0 0	1 0 0	0 0 0	2	7 1
LAD	0 0 1	0 0 0	0 0 0	0 0 0	1 0 0	0 0 1	3	11 1

GAME 3 FRIDAY 10/26/2018 • DODGER STADIUM

BOS	0 0 0	0 0 0	3 1 5	9	8 1
LAD	0 0 0	0 0 4	0 0 2	6	9 0

GAME 4 SATURDAY 10/27/2018 • DODGER STADIUM

BOS	2 0 0	0 0 1	1 1 0	5	8 0
LAD	1 0 0	0 0 0	0 0 0	1	3 0

GAME 5 SUNDAY 10/28/2018 • DODGER STADIUM

BY DAN SHAUGHNESSY • Globe Staff

There'll be no more late October nights watching the Red Sox thrash assorted Yankees, Astros, and Dodgers. The 2018 baseball season is over and the Red Sox are

for the fourth time in 15 seasons. Led by David Price's seven-plus stellar innings and home runs by Steve Pearce (two), Mookie Betts, and J.D. Martinez, the Sox defeated the Dodgers, 5-1, in Dodger Stadium (a.k.a. "Fenway West") to win the 114th Fall Classic in dominant fashion.

So there. New England has another masterpiece for its professional sports High Renaissance.

In the 21st century, we are at 11 championships and counting. Presumably, the Patriots will be going for No. 12 in February, and the Celtics for No. 13 in June. Boylston Street is our Canyon of Heroes.

Staking a claim as one of the greatest teams in baseball history, the 2018 Red Sox finished with 119 wins, including an 11-3 record in the postseason. Matched against the defending world champions (Astros), and two of the game's signature franchises, the Sons of

Alex Cora clinched all three playoff series on the road, shredding the competition by an aggregate 84-51. Pearce, who hit three homers and knocked in seven runs in the final two games, was named World Series MVP.

This is an alternate universe for Sox fans of a certain age. During the 86-year drought, the Red Sox lost the World Series four times, each in an excruciating seventh game. Not anymore. The Red Sox own the World Series in this century, winning in 2004, 2007, 2013, and 2018. The Sox are 16-3 in World Series games in the new millennium.

The Game 5 clincher completed the redemption of David Price, who has been something of a local dartboard ornament since signing a $217 million contract three years ago. Now all is forgiven. After a decade of postseason failure, Price in October '18 won his last three playoff starts, including the clinchers in the ALCS and World

Series. Try to imagine Charlie Brown kicking the game-winning field goal in the Super Bowl. That's what we just saw.

Good grief.

Thousands of Red Sox fans hung around at Dodger Stadium after the final out. They chanted "Yankees suck" before watching the presentation of the Commissioner's Trophy. They cheered madly when Price's image was featured on the jumbo videoboard. They even serenaded the victory platform with a rendition of "Sweet Caroline."

"This is the greatest Red Sox team ever," Sox (and Globe) owner John Henry said after hoisting the trophy.

"What a season!" said Cora, who stood on the same infield as a champion with the Astros (bench coach) last year. "What a way to end it."

Pearce saluted the fans from the victory platform, hollering, "We're world champions, baby!"

world champions

Game 5 featured Clayton Kershaw vs. Price, a duel of veteran southpaws with dubious postseason résumés. Price was the winner with seven innings of three-hit pitching. Joe Kelly came on to strike out the side in the eighth and staff ace Chris Sale did the same in a rare relief appearance in the ninth. Fittingly, postseason bowser Manny Machado fanned on an 0-and-2 pitch to end it at 11:17 Eastern Daylight Time.

The Dodgers were hoping to stave off elimination, send the series back to Fenway Park, and become the eighth team in baseball history to recover from a 3-1 World Series deficit.

No.

In October of 2018, "Beat LA" was more than a chant.

Sunday was LA's Sports Equinox with the Kings, Rams, Galaxy, Ducks, Clippers, and Dodgers all playing home games with starting times spanning from 12:30 to 6:30. All day long, Los Angeles fans complained about Dave Roberts's decision to lift Rich Hill in the seventh inning of Game 4 Saturday night. Hill was working on a 4-0 shutout before Roberts came out with the hook. The Sox scored nine straight runs vs. LA's combustible bullpen and cruised to a 9-6 win. It changed everything in this series and Roberts was ripped by everyone from Mary Hart to President Trump. Roberts may go down in history as a guy who helped win two World Series for the Red Sox: 2004, with his stolen base against Mariano Rivera and the Yankees, and now in 2018, when he pulled Hill from a one-hit shutout.

In Game 5, it didn't take the Sox long to jump ahead. After a one-out single by Andrew Benintendi, Pearce drove Kershaw's sixth pitch over the wall in left-center to make it 2-0. The right side of Dodger Stadium erupted. Clearly, a lot of Dodgers fans had sold their tickets. Matt Damon was among the throng of Sox watchers in the baby-blue ballpark.

Pearce hit his second homer of the night in the eighth; not bad for a 35-year-old journeyman who was acquired by Dave Dombrowski in late June for the immortal Santiago Espinal. Over the final two games, Pearce hit three homers and drove in seven runs.

"This is exactly where we knew we were gonna be," said Pearce. "That's what our team is about. We show up every single day."

On a team with the highest payroll in baseball, a team with Mookie Betts, J.D. Martinez, Chris Sale, and Craig Kimbrel, Steve Pearce was MVP of the World Series. That's the way it went all year with this team. The Sox were loaded with big names and high-priced talent, but the Joe Kellys and Steve Pearces were ever ready when needed.

Gentlemen, start your duck boat engines. The Boston Red Sox are world champions. Again. ■

8-4

W S 1

SALE VS KERSHAW
Eduardo Nunez
celebrates as he
rounds the bases after
his game-clinching
three-run homer in
the seventh inning of
Boston's Series-opening
win. Manny Machado's
sacrifice fly had brought
LA within 5-4 in the
top of the inning before
Nunez connected off
Alex Wood. Managers
Alex Cora and Dave
Roberts, both of whom
played for Boston and
LA, wish each other luck
before the game.

4-2

WS 2

PRICE VS RYU

David Price had plenty of Red Sox defense to shout about in Game 2. He applauded Rafael Devers' play on LA's Chris Taylor in the sixth, and Andrew Benintendi made a leaping, lunging grab of Brian Dozier's liner in the fourth, with the Dodgers leading, 2-1. Boston rallied for three runs in the fifth as five straight men reached base after two were out. J.D. Martinez's two-run single proved the difference.

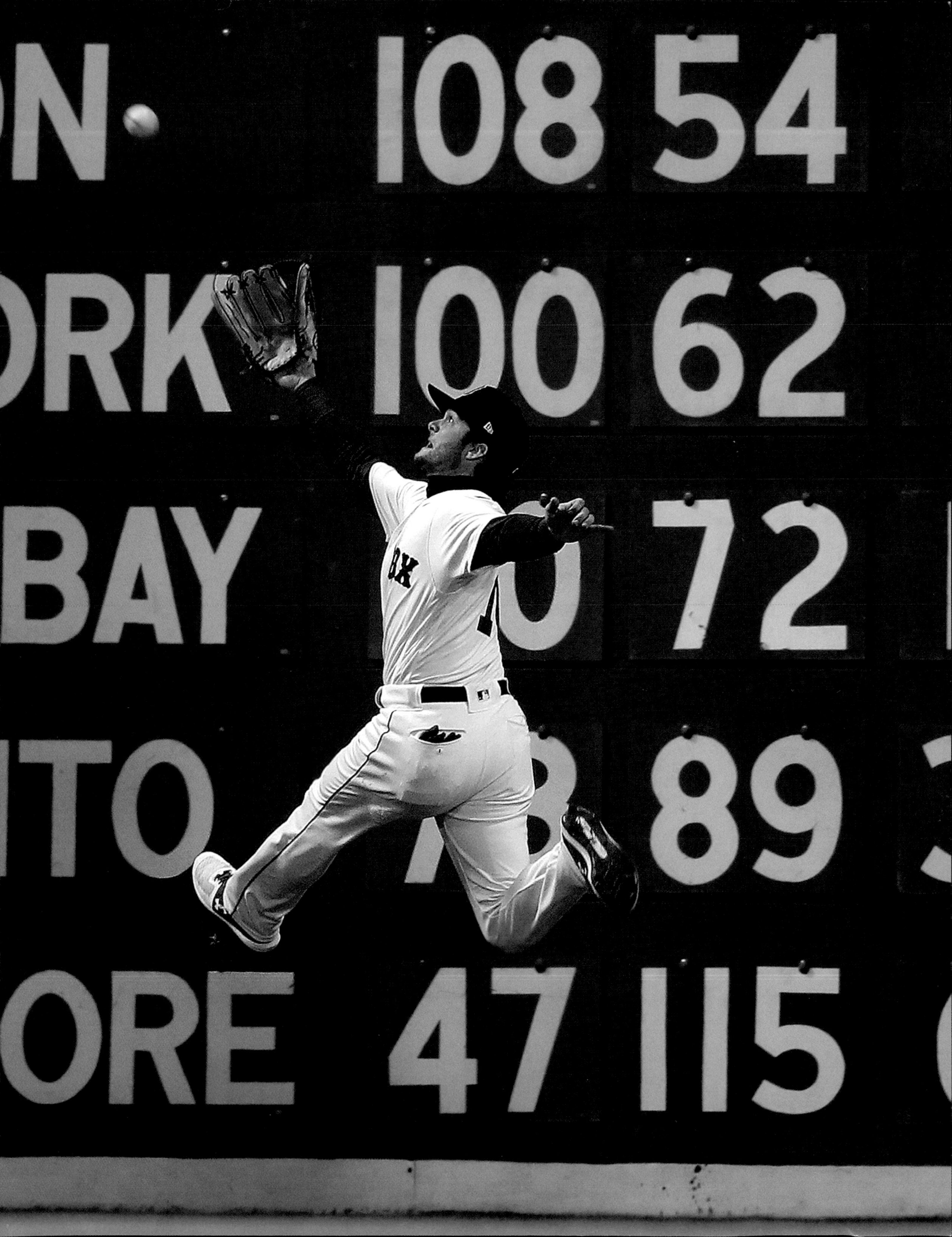
ON 108 54
ORK 100 62
BAY 72
ITO 89
ORE 47 115

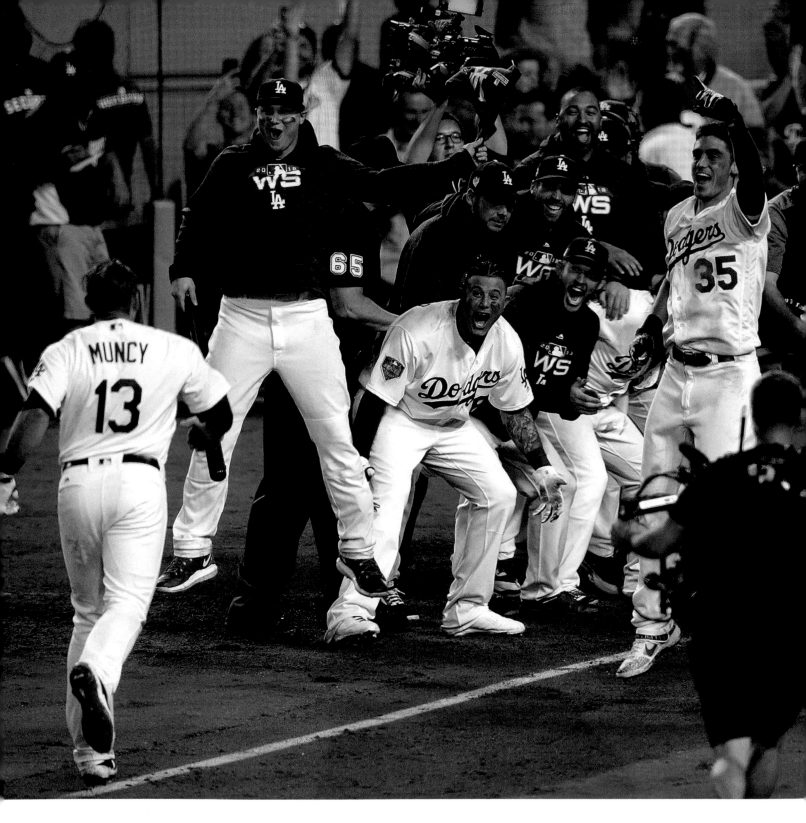

46
Players used by both teams, a record

18
Pitchers used, nine each, most ever in postseason

561
Number of pitches thrown

97
Pitches thrown by Sox reliever Nathan Eovaldi

0-28
Batters 1-4 in Sox lineup had record hitless night

34
Combined strikeouts, a postseason record (Red Sox, 19)

7-0
Dodgers' record in World Series Game 3s at home

2-3

PORCELLO VS BUEHLER

Max Muncy makes his way home through a sea of Dodger blue (far left) after his game-winning homer off Nathan Eovaldi (bottom right) in the 18th inning. Before that (left to right, top to bottom): Manny Machado caught Jackie Bradley Jr. off base; Mookie Betts fanned; a fan fought fatigue in the 17th; J.D. Martinez struck out; Yasiel Puig climbed the wall in vain on Bradley's solo homer; LA catcher Austin Barnes tagged out Ian Kinsler (5), then upended Eduardo Nunez in pursuit of a blocked pitch; Nunez slid into first as Brock Holt scored the go-ahead run; Nunez fell into the seats after catching a foul fly; Kinsler rued his errant, game-tying throw.

Inside 18 innings

In recognition of epic Game 3, the longest game in baseball postseason history, here are some interesting tidbits — and no, that doesn't include the likelihood that the game set a record for most people awake at 3:30 a.m. in Greater Boston:

IT TIED THE 18-INNING NLDS Game 4, won by the Astros over the Braves, as the longest postseason game by innings.

GAME 3 IS THE LONGEST World Series game by 1 hour, 39 minutes over Game 3 in 2005, which went 5 hours, 41 minutes. The White Sox beat the Astros, 7-5, in 14 innings.

THE RED SOX AND DODGERS of 1916 shared the previous record for longest World Series game by innings (14) with that 2005 White Sox-Astros game and Game 1 in 2015 (Royals 5, Mets 4).

THAT BOSTON-BROOKLYN 14-inning game in 1916 was played at Braves Field and took 2 hours, 32 minutes. The Sox won, 2-1, thanks to 13 shutout innings from Babe Ruth.

WHEN LA PITCHER SCOTT ALEXANDER threw high to first base to allow a Boston run in the 13th, it was the first go-ahead run to score on an extra-inning error in the World Series since Mookie Wilson's grounder went between Bill Buckner's legs in Game 6 of 1986.

THE 18 TOTAL PITCHERS USED set a record not only for the World Series, but any postseason game.

NUMBER OF RED SOX PLAYERS who entered the game in the No. 9 spot: 12

RIGHTHANDER NATHAN EOVALDI entered the game in the 12th and threw 97 pitches, becoming the first pitcher to throw 80-plus pitches in relief in a World Series game since Greg Harris in 1984.

GAME 3 LASTED LONGER than the entire 1939 World Series, as the Yankees swept the Reds in four games that lasted a combined 7 hours, 5 minutes.

12:27

NATHAN
EOVALDI
17 · P

2018 Postseason

W/L	ERA	WHIP
2-0	1.21	0.76

INN	BB	SO
22.1	3	16

Game

PITCHES	BALLS	STRIKES
90	32	58

PITCH SPEED / TYPE

MPH

1 for 5

MAX
MUNCY
13 · 2B

2018 Postseason

AVG	HR	RBI	HITS	RUNS
.195	2	5	8	8

OBP	SLG	OPS	OPS+	WAR
.377	.8779	.743	158	

Career

AVG	H	RBI	HR	SLG
.239	146	96	40	.489

SPEED OFF BAT	DISTANCE	LAUNCH ANGLE
MPH	FEET	°

LA DODGERS

57	Wood	P	.000
10	Turner	3B	.283
13	Muncy	2B	.195
8	Machado	SS	.241
35	Bellinger	CF	.130
66	Puig	RF	.302
15	Barnes	C	.083
25	Freese	1B	.353
14	Hernández	LF	.114

Mound Visits Remaining
9

BIOFREEZE
COOL THE PAIN

	10	11	12	13	14	15	16	17	18	R	H	E
	0	0	0	1	0	0	0	0	0	2	7	1
	0	0	0	1	0	0	0	0		2	10	1

Ball	Strike	Out
0	0	0

SAN MANUEL CASINO

9-6

W S 4

RODRIGUEZ VS HILL

Yasiel Puig (66) strikes the game's first big blow, a three-run homer off an exasperated Eduardo Rodriguez in the sixth inning to give LA a 4-0 lead. Mitch Moreland (18) struck back with a three-run pinch-hit homer in the seventh — with two outs, naturally — off the Dodgers' Ryan Madson.

W S 4

Steve Pearce ties Game 4 with an eighth-inning homer, before adding a three-run double in the ninth. Joe Kelly exults after fanning Yasmani Grandal with two men on in the eighth, and Craig Kimbrel could exhale with catcher Blake Swihart after allowing two runs in the ninth.

5-1

W S 5

PRICE VS KERSHAW

David Price allowed a homer to David Freese on his first pitch, then silenced the Dodgers through seven-plus innings as he continued his resounding postseason rebound. In his final three postseason starts, Price was 3-0 with a 1.42 ERA in 19 innings, allowing 9 hits and 5 walks with 19 strikeouts. Said manager Alex Cora of Price, "[Every day] there was a text, 'I'm ready for tomorrow. Count on me. Use me.'"

Series MVP Steve Pearce hits a two-run homer, his first of two round-trippers, in the top of the first, and Mookie Betts ends an 0-for-12 drought with a solo shot in the sixth inning. Pearce had three homers and a three-run double, driving in seven runs, in his final six at-bats of the World Series.

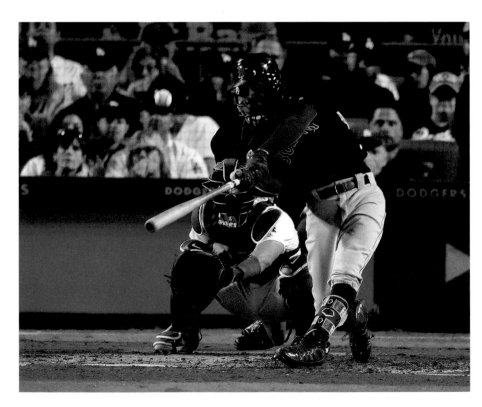

J.D. Martinez, obviously hampered by an ankle injury he sustained running the bases in Game 1, provides insurance for Boston with a solo homer in the seventh inning. Christian Vazquez is quickly out of his crouch after Manny Machado went down swinging for the Dodgers' final out.

Pennant
resilient

2-7

									R	H	E
HOU	0	2	0	0	0	1	0	0	4	7	5	1
BOS	0	0	0	0	2	0	0	0	0	2	3	1

GAME 1 SATURDAY 10/13/2018 • FENWAY PARK

7-5

										R	H	E
HOU	0	2	2	0	0	0	0	0	1	5	7	1
BOS	2	0	3	0	0	0	1	1	x	7	9	0

GAME 2 SUNDAY 10/14/2018 • FENWAY PARK

8-2

										R	H	E
BOS	2	0	0	0	0	1	0	5	0	8	9	0
HOU	1	0	0	0	1	0	0	0	0	2	7	0

GAME 3 TUESDAY 10/16/2018 • MINUTE MAID PARK

8-6

										R	H	E
BOS	2	0	1	0	1	2	1	1	0	8	11	1
HOU	0	1	2	1	1	0	0	1	0	6	13	0

GAME 4 WEDNESDAY 10/17/2018 • MINUTE MAID PARK

4-1

										R	H	E
BOS	0	0	1	0	0	3	0	0	0	4	8	0
HOU	0	0	0	0	0	0	1	0	0	1	5	1

GAME 5 THURSDAY 10/18/2018 • MINUTE MAID PARK

Jackie Bradley Jr. embraces Andrew Benintendi after Benintendi snagged the game-ending — and game-saving — catch on a sinking liner by the Astros' Alex Bregman in Boston's 8-6 Game 4 win.

BY DAN SHAUGHNESSY • Globe Staff

The relentless Red Sox won
on Oct. 18, beating the defending world champion Houston Astros

4-1, in Game 5 of the American League Championship Series.

And here are the words you thought you'd never read: The Red Sox clinched the pennant on the strength of six innings of stellar, pressure-packed pitching from the much-maligned David Price. That's right. On three days' rest, filling in for ace Chris Sale, matched up against one of the best postseason pitchers of this generation (Justin Verlander), Price hurled six shutout innings, giving up three hits, striking out nine, and walking none. In the most important game of his Red Sox career, Price finally won a postseason start. It was his first scoreless outing in 12 playoff starts and he did it after warming up feverishly in the eighth and ninth innings of an epic Game 4 Red Sox victory.

"One of the most special days I've ever had on a baseball field," Price said as he held his young son in his lap at the postgame podium. "So I'm very excited ... It's very special for all of us. It's something that AC [manager Alex Cora] talked about in spring training ... To do what we did in New York and to beat the reigning champs. That was very special for all of us ... I definitely felt good on the mound. Continued to tell myself to stay in the moment. I was able to do that tonight."

"He's never going to forget it," said ALCS MVP Jackie Bradley Jr. "I know I'm not."

"I don't want to pick battles in the media," said Cora. "But I was watching a show this morning on MLB Network and it was embarrassing the way they were talking about David Price and I was offended by that ...That one got me. When he was throwing 94 tonight, I thought of that."

Wow. In Nixonian fashion, I must ask, "What will we do now that we don't have David Price to kick around anymore?"

The near-biblical redemption of David Price is a better local sports story than the redemption of John Lackey in 2013. Shoot, it's probably a better tale than "The Shawshank Redemption." Price has been our local hard-ball pinata since he signed a $217 million contract with the Sox three years ago. He's been widely mocked as a softie, addicted to Fortnite, armed with excuses, and unable to perform in the clutch. He hit rock bottom when he verbally ambushed the beloved Dennis Eckersley in the summer of 2017, then refused to apologize.

Meanwhile, his postseason failures have been memorialized like "The Midnight Ride of Paul Revere." In the first 11 starts of his postseason career, Price went 0-9. In his first 19 overall playoff appearances he was 2-9 with a 5.42 ERA. In a sport that worships Mr. October, Mr. Price was Mr. May, Mr. June, and Mr. July.

Then came Game 5 against the world champs at Minute Maid Park. There seemed little chance that

the pennant

any game could live up to the drama we saw in Game 4, a 4-hour-33-minute epic that ended after 1 a.m. (EDT). The baseball world was still buzzing about Andrew Benintendi's game-saving catch when the teams gathered for Game 5.

The Verlander-Price matchup featured a duel of former Tigers teammates and former Cy Young winners.

It also was a joust of two men with entirely different postseason reputations.

Verlander is Mr. Elimination Game. One of the most accomplished postseason pitchers in history, Mr. Kate Upton came into the night with a streak of 24 scoreless innings in games in which his team had to win or go home. He extended that streak to 26 before J.D. Martinez took him over the wall in the third.

Price came into the game with the George Costanza Bizarro World opposite reputation. Price was so historically bad in the playoffs, he was practically hoisted on the shoulders of his teammates after struggling (four runs, five hits, four walks) for 4 2/3 innings of his start against the Astros on Oct. 14. When Price left that game with a lead,

and the Sox went on to win, it was something of a breakthrough.

Game 5 was a House Money game for Price and birthday boy Cora (43). Knowing Boston would be facing Verlander, Cora emptied his vault in Game 4. Sweat-soaked closer Craig Kimbrel staggered through his first six-out save of the year, Price warmed up throughout the eighth and ninth, and Cora was prepared to make Game 5 a bullpen game if necessary. With three chances to win once, facing Verlander in Houston in this match up, it seemed like a sound strategy.

Led by Cowboy Joe West — New England's new Walt Coleman — the six MLB umpires were loudly booed when they came out for the pregame exchange of lineup cards.

With one out in the third, Martinez launched a 1-and-2 breaking ball far over the left field fence. It was a no-doubter. Even for West.

Price got into a groove after the second. He struck out the side in the fourth and got the Astros 1-2-3 in the fifth. After baby-faced Rafael Devers made it 4-0 with a three-run homer in the sixth, Price got the side in order again in the bottom of the inning. He retired the last seven

batters he faced and turned the 4-0 lead over to the bullpen in the seventh.

"It was good in the bullpen warming up and it got better as the game went on," said Price.

"It shows the competitor that he is," said Bradley.

"You can talk about the David Price struggles all you want," said Houston manager A.J. Hinch. "He's been tough on us. And that was as hard as we've seen him throw against us. You could tell how much it meant to him."

Matt Barnes surrendered a homer to Marwin Gonzalez, but Nathan Eovaldi and Kimbrel cleaned up the final 2 1/3 innings and it was time for yet another champagne bath.

David Price and the Red Sox were on their way to the World Series. ■

14 PENNANTS

2-7

A L C S 1

SALE VS VERLANDER
Clockwise from left, Chris Sale struggled with his control, allowing two runs on one hit, with four walks in four innings. J.D. Martinez doesn't like the strike call in the eighth. Manager Alex Cora pleads his case in the fifth, and Andrew Benintendi reacts after striking out in the fourth. Houston broke it open with four runs in the ninth.

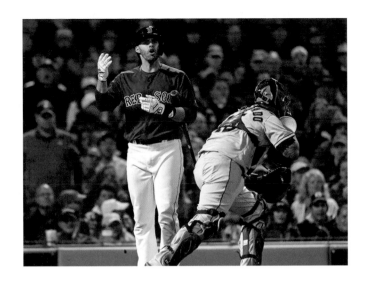

7-5

PRICE VS COLE
Houston left fielder
Marwin Gonzalez chases
a ball that dances along
the ledge near the foul
line for a three-run
double by Jackie Bradley
Jr., giving Boston a 5-4
lead in the third inning.
Boston's bullpen threw
3 1/3 hitless innings until
the ninth, when Craig
Kimbrel struggled to a
shaky one-run save.

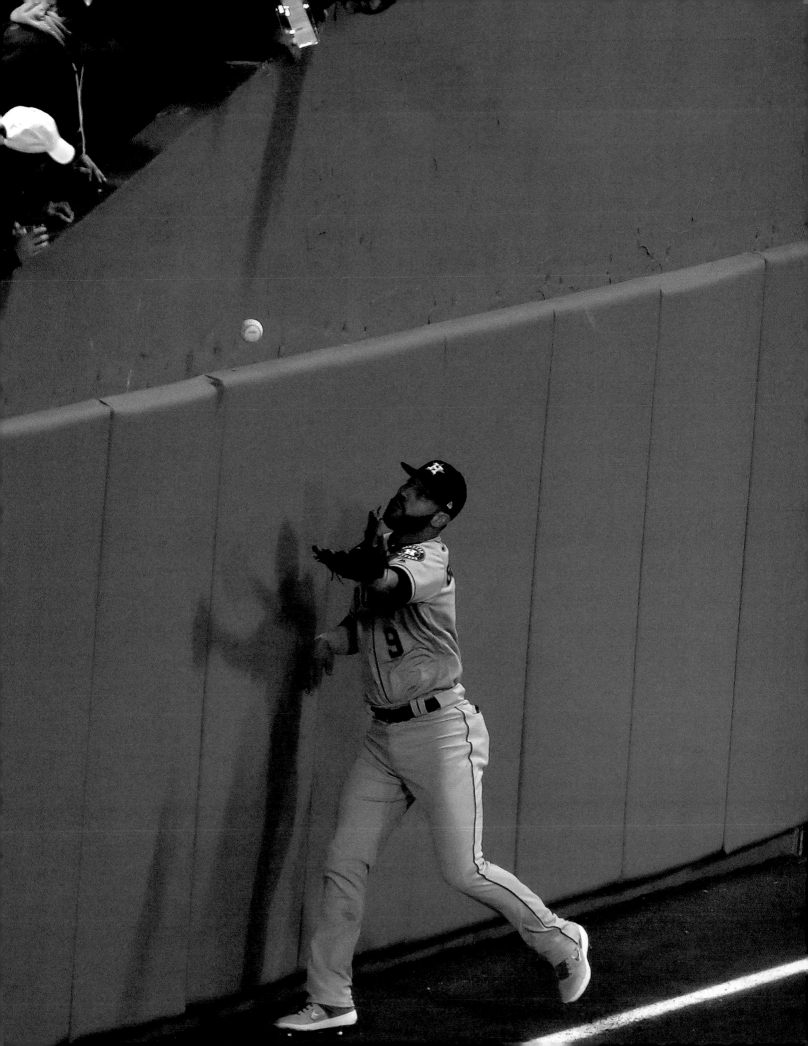

8-2

ALCS 3

EOVALDI VS KEUCHEL

Nathan Eovaldi threw six innings of two-run ball and earned his second win of the postseason, thanks to Steve Pearce (right), who crushed a solo home run in the top of the sixth off the Astros' Joe Smith to give the Red Sox a 3-2 lead.

One word says it all

RELENTLESS.

Defined in the dictionary as "oppressively constant; incessant; unrelenting." Defined on the baseball field by the 2018 Boston Red Sox. Like waves crashing onto the beach, retreating and regrouping to do it all again, undeterred by any obstacles, so do these Red Sox churn. Bad loss? No problem. Get the next one. That's what the Red Sox did after losing Game 2 of the Division Series at home to the Yankees, and what they did again after losing Game 1 of the AL Championship Series at home to the Astros.

Bad at-bat? No worries. Let the next guy do it. That's what they did in handing the ALCS MVP trophy to Jackie Bradley Jr., who usually bats last in their order.

They never stop. They are relentless.

Astros manager A.J. Hinch, who led his team to a World Series championship a year ago, couldn't stop using the word in the aftermath of this year's failed attempt to defend that title, when his major league-best pitching staff proved no match for a Red Sox lineup that wore it to shreds, when his own hitters couldn't manage to dent a Red Sox bullpen that was suspect all year, when the Red Sox' stellar defense stole outs with leaping catches by Mookie Betts and sliding ones by Andrew Benintendi, when even embattled Red Sox starter David Price joined the party by pitching a gem in the clinching Game 5.

This was Hinch after that game: "They have the most wins in the league for a reason. ... They have tremendous balance. They put pressure on you from the very beginning. They don't concede any at-bats.

"And then when people doubted them, you know, it seemed like they got better. And they never stopped. They never stopped coming at you. They're a relentless group."

It's not an easy quality to quantify, nor is it possible to bottle it up. But it is contagious.

"They're playing with a sense of urgency the whole postseason," manager Alex Cora said before Game 1 of the World Series. "Starters, relievers, position players, we like to use the expression, 'We're all in.' And they are. They are all in. That's cool to see."

For fans, yes. For opponents? Exhausting. ■

TARA SULLIVAN

ALCS 3

Jackie Bradley Jr. follows the flight of his victory-clinching grand slam off Houston's Roberto Osuna in the eighth inning of Game 3. The blast came with two outs and followed consecutive hit batters by Osuna, one of which drove in a run.

BY ALEX SPEIER • Globe Staff

What's the second base shimmy?

Mystery surrounds a late-season Red Sox development.

"Honestly, I don't know how it started," said Brock Holt.

"That's just something that you're going to have to talk to [Andrew] Benintendi about," deflected Ian Kinsler.

"You've been misinformed. I have no answers," countered Benintendi. "I can't give details."

While the origins remain obscure — either unknown or carefully protected — a new trend was sweeping across the Red Sox by September of this year, and it had little to do with launch angle, spin rate, or first-pitch breaking balls. For the first time since Celtics forward Antoine Walker, "the shimmy" was becoming a thing for a Boston pro sports team.

While some Red Sox players were under the impression that the celebratory shake of the hips with arms extended parallel to the ground originated in late August, during the seven-game road trip through Chicago and then Atlanta, Holt accurately noted that the enthusiastic observance of a double predated the trip. After the lineup endured a

fallow stretch in mid-August against the Phillies and Rays, the team recognized a need to alter its mix.

"We were talking about that today, 'How did we start doing that?' The little shimmy thing, I honestly don't know how it started. I think someone said we needed to change things up because we weren't doing things for extra-base hits," said Holt. "Mookie [Betts] hit a double the other night in that big inning and did it, and I think it reminded all of us ... Then I hit the triple and did it, then Blake [Swihart] did it, and it became a thing after that."

Holt's description allows for a fairly efficient investigation. The "big inning" in question was the 11-run, seventh-inning eruption in a 14-6 victory over the Marlins at Fenway on Aug. 29. Clearly, going 12 for 13 in an inning can serve as a catalyst for a movement, with Holt's recollection proving accurate — Betts, Holt, and Swihart did indeed shimmy after their extra-base hits that inning.

For the most part, the display follows a double. However, the team is willing to make exceptions.

"Throw it in there every once in a while, no matter where ... You just kind of do whatever," Benintendi detailed. "There's really no rules."

Steve Pearce, for instance, was beaming when he received a call to shimmy after a bases-loaded single in the 5-1 victory over the Braves on Sept. 4. He was more than happy to comply with the request.

"They were signaling me to do it. I look in the dugout and everyone was going, 'Let's go! Let's get it done!'" said Pearce. "It's sort of a momentum thing, a way to have fun and keep it light. That's kind of what we want out there. We're out there having fun. You're having fun on the field, and the results have been good."

At a time when the 140-game toll of a season tends to weigh on players, the Red Sox suggest that their delight in a simple celebration is an expression of the joy of a season.

"It's fun, man. This team is fun," said Holt. "We've got a lot of good players. We've had fun since Day 1 of spring training. Everyone gets along, everyone roots for each other, and little things like that — the season is long. That kind of shortens it a little bit, lets us have fun together, and gets the guys in the dugout going a little bit, too. It keeps everyone in the game and we're having a really good time."

The Red Sox represent something of a rarity in today's game, a team capable of building and sustaining rallies not just on the strength of the long ball but instead with a diverse array of offensive tools — old-school rallies featuring hit after hit, double after double, and, of course, shimmy after shimmy.

"I don't know who started it," said Pearce, "but we're going to keep it rolling." ■

8-6

A L C S 4

PORCELLO VS MORTON

A fan trying to catch a fly ball off the bat of Houston's Jose Altuve hampers Mookie Betts in his attempt to make the catch in the first inning of Game 4. Umpire Joe West ruled Altuve out on fan interference, possibly costing the Astros two runs. Umpires huddle to discuss, and it's ruled that the call on the field stands.Houston later rallied to take the lead, 5-4, but the bullpen failed to hold the Red Sox at bay.

Tony Kemp of the Astros is tagged out by Xander Bogaerts on a stellar throw by Boston right fielder Mookie Betts as Kemp attempted to stretch an eighth-inning single.

Spygate,
version 2.0

THE HOUSTON ASTROS

are the New England Patriots. They win a championship, and everyone thinks they're cheating.

The 2018 American League Championship Series took on a new dimension when the Boston Metro first reported that a guy with a camera working for the Astros was kicked out of the photographers well by the first base dugout at Fenway Park during Game 1. Turns out the same guy got the heave-ho in Cleveland when the 'Stros were beating up on the Tribe in the Division Series.

Perfect. Spygate comes to baseball. Next thing you know the Astros will be accused of deflating baseballs.

In the middle of all this, we have Red Sox manager Alex Cora, who last year won a championship with the Astros. The Astros evidently think he's ratting them out now that he's trying to beat Houston with his new team. I am not the first to conclude that this makes Cora the new Eric Mangini.

You remember Mangini, right? Won a ring with the Patriots, was hired away by the New York Jets, then told NFL security about Bill Belichick's camera tricks. The Jets caught the Patriots videotaping coaches' signals at the Meadowlands and a price was paid. Mangini became dead to Bill, as in "I knew it was you, Fredo. You broke my heart."

Boston's baseball bosses want MLB to come at the Astros with the full fury of Arlen Specter and Marshall Faulk, but it needs to be said that the Sox are not without sin in these matters. Just last year they were fined by MLB after they were caught in a relay scheme involving video folks text-messaging a team trainer.

MLB said it was going to crack down "next time." But that did not happen. MLB issued a short statement on Oct. 18, clearing the Astros of wrongdoing and stating that it considers the case closed.

So there. No Wells Report. No $1 million fine. No loss of a first-round draft pick. No 20-game suspension for Justin Verlander at the start of next season.

Where's Judge Richard Berman when we need him? ◼

DAN SHAUGHNESSY

A L C S 4

Red Sox left fielder Andrew Benintendi displays the ball to the umpire after making a spectacular sliding grab of a sinking liner by Houston's Alex Bregman to preserve Boston's 8-6 victory in Game 4.

4-1

PRICE VS VERLANDER
David Price pitches in
the first inning of what
would become his
best-ever postseason
outing. Price improved
to 1-9 as a starter by
scattering three hits over
six scoreless innings,
walking none and
striking out nine. Craig
Kimbrel allowed one
walk in a one-inning save
that sent the Red Sox on
to the World Series.

A L C S 5

J.D. Martinez gave
Boston a 1-0 lead with
his third-inning homer
off Justin Verlander,
and Rafael Devers
provided insurance
with an opposite-
field, three-run homer
in the sixth inning.

A L C S 5

Red Sox right fielder Mookie Betts catches a fly ball off the bat of the Astros' Alex Bregman near the right-field wall in the sixth inning of Game 5 at Minute Maid Park. The play was a near do-over of the Game 4 moment when Betts and the Red Sox benefited from a fan interference ruling in the first inning of the 8-6 win. This time, however, no umpire was needed to make the call.

DIVISION
rivalry changing

Yankees

5-4

		1	2	3		4	5	6		7	8	9		R	H	E
NY		0	0	0		0	0	2		1	0	1		4	10	0
BOS		3	0	2		0	0	0		0	0	x		5	8	0

GAME 1 FRIDAY 10/5/2018 • **FENWAY PARK**

2-6

		1	2	3		4	5	6		7	8	9		R	H	E
NY		1	2	0		0	0	0		3	0	0		6	8	0
BOS		0	0	0		1	0	0		1	0	0		2	5	1

GAME 2 SATURDAY 10/6/2018 • **FENWAY PARK**

16-1

		1	2	3		4	5	6		7	8	9		R	H	E
BOS		0	1	2		7	0	0		1	3	2		16	18	0
NY		0	0	0		1	0	0		0	0	0		1	5	0

GAME 3 MONDAY 10/8/2018 • **YANKEE STADIUM**

4-3

		1	2	3		4	5	6		7	8	9		R	H	E
BOS		0	0	3		1	0	0		0	0	0		4	8	0
NY		0	0	0		0	1	0		0	0	2		3	5	1

GAME 4 TUESDAY 10/9/2018 • **YANKEE STADIUM**

After their team lost Game 1, Yankee fans await the start of Game 2 of the AL Division Series at Fenway Park.

BY DAN SHAUGHNESSY • Globe Staff

On Oct. 3, Yankee Stadium fans were chanting "We want

while the Yanks were beating the Oakland A's in the one-game wild-card playoff.

They got Boston.

With both barrels.

And full fury.

Less than a week later, the Sox beat the Yankees, 4-3, winning their American League Division Series, 3-1, to advance to the ALCS.

After finishing first in three straight seasons, the 108-win Red Sox won the franchise's first playoff series since that championship season of 2013.

The final moments of the ALDS were frightening and downright weird. It was Clinchus Interruptus. The game ended on a groundout to third, but the Sox couldn't celebrate until the play was reviewed at MLB's replay center. So the Sox stood around the infield, waited for the review, then tossed their gloves in the air. It was like pushing your out-of-gas car across the finish line to win the Indianapolis 500.

Boston led 4-1 when the bottom of the ninth started. Craig Kimbrel, a Hall-of-Fame-bound closer, came on to slam the door. Perfect, right? A clean inning. A three-run lead. All the momentum in the world.

And then it almost all unraveled. Walk. Single. Strikeout. Walk. Hit by pitch to force in a run. A high fly by Gary Sanchez that might have been out of Fenway but was a mere sac fly at Yankee Stadium that cut the lead to 4-3.

With the tying and winning runs aboard, rookie Gleyber Torres hit a weak chopper to third. Eduardo Nunez charged, pocketed the ball, and fired to first, barely beating Torres.

But it was not perfectly clear. As the Sox started to celebrate, the Yankees challenged the call. While this was going on, Nunez appeared to hurt himself while starting the celebration. A trainer came out to look at Nunez while the umps gathered to look at the play. Finally, the out signal was given and the Sox resumed their celebration. Weird.

It was like the end of the 2016 season when the Sox clinched the American League East while the Yankees were batting in the bottom of the ninth. The Sox clinched only because the Orioles beat the Blue Jays. After learning they had clinched, Kimbrel loaded the bases and Joe Kelly surrendered a walkoff grand slam to Mark Teixeira. So

we saw both teams celebrating simultaneously at the end of the game. In the Sox clubhouse, manager John Farrell had to prod his players to pop the bubbly.

This division win was similarly awkward.

But who cares? The Sox moved on. They played Sinatra's "New York, New York" while dousing one another with champagne in the visitors' clubhouse.

There was an air of desperation on 161st Street in the moments before Game 4. Teetering on the brink of elimination after their own 100-win season, the Yankees rolled out Bucky Dent for the ceremonial first pitch.

Ha-ha. These guys never stop. It's not enough that they've got Aaron Bleepin' Boone in the dugout? They've got to summon Bucky Bleepin' Dent for a first pitch? Why not introduce the great grandson of Harry Frazee?

The stunt didn't work in 2004 when Dent was called in to stop the bleeding before Game 7 at the old Yankee Stadium. That was the same night that the Yanks assigned Sox ownership to the Babe Ruth suite. There was no Bucky/Bambino magic. The Sox scored six in the first

Boston!"

two innings, won 10-3, and danced on the Yankee lawn, celebrating the greatest comeback in baseball history.

And now Boston has done it to New York again.

Coming into this series, the Yanks liked their chances at home. They had won seven consecutive playoff games at the new Yankee Stadium, including four elimination games in 2017. But the raging Red Sox pummeled the Yankees, 20-4, over 18 innings in the House of Steinbrenner.

Sweet. For all their success over the last three seasons, the Sox had been unable to win a playoff series, and there were doubts about their chances in this first-round matchup after they were beaten by the Yankees, 6-2, in Game 2 at Fenway. Boston's bullpen was a mess, David Price was rendered useless, and Yankee slugger Aaron Judge was taunting the Sox with Sinatra's "New York, New York."

It was then that rookie manager Alex Cora shifted into genius mode — making all the right moves as the Sox mowed down the Bronx Bombers on their own sacred sod. Dick Williams steered the Impossible Dream Red Sox to a World Series

in 1967 and Tito Francona won two crowns in his eight seasons at Fenway, but it would be hard to find a Sox skipper with a hotter hand than Cora's.

He went to four bench guys in Game 3 and they all produced (Brock Holt hit for the cycle). He predicted Nathan Eovaldi would throw seven innings and give up one run in Game 3. He let Christian Vazquez catch Rick Porcello for the first time all season in Game 4 and Vazquez hit a homer as Porcello picked up his first career playoff win. In the eighth inning of Game 4, Cora went off the grid and summoned ace lefty Chris Sale for his first relief appearance since last year's playoffs. Sale retired the side in order on 13 pitches.

"A lot of people gave up on us after losing Game 2," said Cora. "We showed up last night and tonight had our plan mapped out. At the end, he wasn't the usual Craig Kimbrel, but he got three outs."

It's safe to say that there is a new world order in this ancient rivalry. After sucking exhaust for eight decades — an 86-year stretch in which the Yankees won 26 World Series to Boston's zero — the Sox have become kings of the American

League in this century, winning four World Series to New York's one.

The tide turned in 2004 when Francona's Red Sox shocked the world and beat the Yankees after trailing three games to none. Oct. 9, 2018 marked the fourth time the Sox have sipped champagne here since '04.

Finally, the Sox are the Yankees' daddies.

Feels good, doesn't it? ∎

DIVISION TITLES

5-4

ALDS 1

SALE VS HAPP

Having lost the ALDS opener the previous two years, the Red Sox got off to a rollicking start with a three-run homer from J.D. Martinez (left). Chris Sale, who had pitched just 17 innings since July 27, left in the sixth with a 5-0 lead. But the bullpen allowed two inherited runners to score, and the Yankees made it close in the ninth.

2-6

ALDS 2

PRICE VS TANAKA

Postseason woes persisted for David Price (right) as the Red Sox starter left in the second inning after allowing three runs on just five outs. Gary Sanchez (24) celebrated his second homer of the night, a mammoth three-run shot off Eduardo Rodriguez that broke open a 3-2 game. Aaron Judge (far left), homered for the second straight night.

16-1

A L D S 3

EOVALDI VS SEVERINO

Brock Holt celebrates his ninth-inning homer in Boston's 16-1 win, which set the record for the most lopsided road victory in baseball postseason history. Boston drove Yankee ace Luis Severino (top right) from the game in a seven-run fourth inning. Andrew Benintendi (second right) had a three-run double. Nathan Eovaldi (third right) went seven strong innings for the win, and Mookie Betts rounded third base on the way to Boston's seventh run of the game in the fourth inning.

Making Brocktober history

BROCK HOLT was ready when the opportunity was presented to him.

After he sat out the first two games of the American League Division Series against the Yankees, Holt made history in Game 3, becoming the first player ever to hit for the cycle in a playoff game, amassing a single, double, triple, and homer as part of a 4-for-6 game in which he drove in five runs and scored three times.

Holt grounded out in his first plate appearance, but bounced back with a single (against Yankees starter Luis Severino to lead off the fourth inning and set in motion a seven-run frame by the Red Sox), a two-run triple (also in the fourth inning, this time against reliever Chad Green), and a run-scoring double (eighth inning against lefty Stephen Tarpley).

Given one last opportunity to hit when Ian Kinsler walked with two outs in the top of the ninth, Holt blasted a 79-wmile-per-hour, first-pitch offering from Yankees catcher-turned-mop-up man Austin Romine into the seats down the right field line for his roundtripper.

That blast made him the first player ever to hit for the cycle in October, though Holt had done it once before in the regular season. ▪

ALEX SPEIER

4-3

A L D S 4

PORCELLO VS SABATHIA

Red Sox first baseman Steve Pearce snares the ball for the final out of Game 4 — and the series. Boston took a 4-1 lead into the ninth, thanks in part to a strong effort from starter Rick Porcello and three early runs off C.C. Sabathia. Boston closer Craig Kimbrel again struggled, allowing two runs before finally closing the door on New York's season.

BY STAN GROSSFELD • Globe Staff

Bullpen cop bids adieu

When Detroit Tigers outfielder Torii Hunter went head-first into the Red Sox bullpen during a playoff game in 2013, Boston police officer Steve Horgan became the most famous bullpen cop on the planet.

Nearly five years after David Ortiz's grand slam, he is still joyously re-creating his touchdown pose, which has become a famous Boston sports photo. Fans still line up before every game to get selfies taken with Horgan.

That won't happen anymore because the 33-year veteran is retiring.

"I feel it's just time to move on," he said in a Fenway Park interview interrupted several times by fans raising their arms.

"I want to pursue cooking. The first thing I want to do is go to the King Arthur Baking School and learn how to make bread properly."

So this season was last call for Horgan selfies. He estimates he has taken 25,000 of them. He always poses with his right hand open and his left hand closed, just like in the picture.

"I try to be authentic," he said. "I had salt and pepper sunflower seeds in my hand and I didn't want to drop them."

It was the eighth inning of Game 2 of the American League Championship Series, and the Sox were trailing, 5-1, and in danger of falling into a two-game deficit against the Tigers.

But Big Papi had other ideas. His home run started the Sox on the way to a World Series title.

Ortiz smashed a Joaquin Benoit changeup toward the bullpen, and Hunter, the right fielder, went full throttle for the ball, which was up in the lights and curving away from him.

First the ball, then Hunter, landed in the Sox bullpen. Hard.

"I think that if that wall wasn't in his way he would have caught it," Horgan said. "But the wall was in the way."

The image — Hunter's legs in the air next to Horgan's raised arms — is one of Boston's iconic sports moments, like Bobby Orr flying through the air to win the 1970 Stanley Cup or Carlton Fisk waving his 1975 World Series home run fair.

It was a Boston Strong moment that helped heal a city stung by the Boston Marathon bombings in April of that year.

"It was joyous," said Horgan, who was invited to ride on the duck boats after the Sox won the World Series.

Horgan was born in Dorchester and said he's been a Red Sox fan from birth. He started coming to Fenway when a bleacher seat cost a dollar. In those days, his mother sent him to the ballpark with a can of Pepsi wrapped in tinfoil to stay cold. He loved Yaz and the Spaceman and passing the time at the old yard with his father.

Horgan landed the gig in the bullpen in 2013 (the assignment is usually at the discretion of the District 4 captain) after covering traffic outside Fenway Park since 2004. He had routinely celebrated Red Sox home runs, but "nobody noticed," he said.

That changed when Hunter went head over heels.

The bullpen cop has been Photoshopped onto the deck of the Titanic, descending Splash Mountain, and signaling a Patriots touchdown. He's even been recognized at Wrigley Field in plain clothes.

Horgan is not just a bullpen cop. He rode on the Boston Police mounted unit until it was disbanded in 2009.

On Marathon Monday in 2013, Horgan was stationed on Dartmouth Street between Newbury and Boylston streets. He heard and felt the first explosion. As others ran away, he and fellow

officer Tommy Antonino raced toward the scene.

"He is one of the most humble individuals that I've ever met," said Boston Police Commissioner William Gross said. "You would think that he would get kind of jaded or, like, grumpy. But not once did he ever deny anyone a picture."

The players like him, too.

When the Red Sox won the 2013 World Series, bullpen cop Steve Horgan took a bow. His five years of fame, which he never takes for granted, stem from being at the right place with the right sign.

Craig Kimbrel always shakes his hand. Said bullpen catcher Mani Martinez, "Sometimes I play with him and say, 'Wow, you're really famous,' and he says, 'I'm not really famous. I'm popular.'" ■

Season
remarkable

Alex Cora greets his players at Tropicana Field in St. Petersburg, Fla., after the Red Sox were announced on Opening Day, Cora's first as a manager.

MARCH/APRIL

21-7

After losing on Opening Day, the Sox win 17 of their next 18 games to become just the seventh team since 1900 to start 17-2. They hit an MLB record-tying six grand slams in April and win a team-record 19 games.

MAY

18-11

The Yankees match the Red Sox with their own 17-1 run and briefly lead the AL East (26-10 to 25-11), but Boston wins 9 of its last 11 of the month for a 39-18 record and a 2-game lead.

JUNE

17-10

The Red Sox assume the division lead for good on June 27, holding the top spot for all but 12 days of the season. Chris Sale caps the month with 11 strikeouts in an 11-0 win over the Yankees.

2018
AMERICAN LEAGUE EAST

	W	L	%	GB
Boston	108	54	.667	
New York	100	62	.617	8
Tampa Bay	90	72	.556	18
Toronto	73	89	.451	35
Baltimore	47	115	.290	61

Having taken the league by storm, Mookie Betts takes the field in a game against the Angels on June 28.

JULY

19-6

After losing their first game of July, the Sox go on a 15-2 tear, triggered by Rick Porcello's 3-run double and victory over Max Scherzer at Nationals Park. They outscore opponents by 3 runs a game during the streak (106-56).

AUGUST

18-9

The Sox start the month with a four-game home sweep of the Yankees to extend their division lead to 9½ games. They would never lead by fewer than 6 games the rest of the season.

SEPTEMBER

15-11

The Red Sox extend their advantage to a season-high 11½ games on Sept. 16, and clinch the division on Sept. 20 with an 11-6 win at Yankee Stadium, fittingly sealed by MVP candidate Mookie Betts' 3-run homer.

BY NICK CAFARDO • Globe Staff

IT HAS BECOME A SPRING TRAINING ritual for the Red Sox to gather every player and coach in a room before the first full-squad workout to be introduced to staff members and hear a few speeches designed to set the tone for the coming season.

When new manager Alex Cora presided over what he called the "company meeting" on Feb. 20, he changed the usual agenda.

Instead of the people who work in community relations, fan services, media relations, and other ancillary departments being asked to leave once they were introduced, they were invited to stay.

Cora's message was that the Sox were more than 25 players,

that every person who worked for the team would be needed for the franchise to win the World Series.

"That day resonated with a lot of people," right fielder Mookie Betts said. "He wanted everybody to take ownership of what they did. We were all part of the same crew. Everybody was working toward the same goal."

That meeting was one of the first examples of how Cora brought change to the Red Sox and turned what was a good team under former manager John Farrell into a historically great one.

The Red Sox won for the 106th time on Sept. 24, breaking a team record set 106 years ago. For the first time since 1946, they entered the postseason with sole possession of the best record in baseball.

Betts had become a leading candidate for Most Valuable Player of the American League, a legitimate challenger to Mike Trout as the best player in the sport.

J.D. Martinez hit for average and power, his numbers reminiscent of David Ortiz in his prime.

Recalcitrant lefthander David Price found at least temporary favor with the fans with one of the best seasons of his career, carrying the rotation when ace Chris Sale spent much of the summer on the disabled list.

The last time the Red Sox were this dominant, in 1912, the Titanic sank the first week of the season, Fenway Park was brand new, and their manager, Jake Stahl, was the son of a Civil War veteran.

"It's something where we should call time out and enjoy this one," Cora said after the record-setting victory on Sept. 24. "For this to happen is very special."

It is what the Sox were seeking when they made the unusual decision to fire Farrell after back-to-back AL East championships and 93-win seasons.

President of baseball operations Dave Dombrowski felt the atmosphere around the team was stifling the young players and a new manager and coaching staff were needed.

Cora, the 43-year-old Houston Astros bench coach, had the inclusive personality to pull the team together. That he had played for the Red Sox and worked as an analyst for ESPN made him an even better fit for the job.

Cora had never managed in the majors, but that was almost incidental. More importantly, he would be the first minority manager in team history. The Sox were ready for significant change.

"People feel comfortable around him," Dombrowski said. "He's been very good. It's a tough job, it's a big job, and he does it very well. The communication is there with everybody."

It wasn't only the clubhouse that changed. Cora transformed how the Sox played. A team that once valued working deep into counts and making the opposing pitcher work became more aggressive at the plate.

The Sox led the majors in runs and slugging percentage. They were even third overall in stolen bases.

Cora and new hitting coach Tim Hyers prodded shortstop Xander Bogaerts into hitting for more power, convincing the modest 25-year-old that he is one of the best players at his position in the game.

The coaches revamped the approach of center fielder Jackie Bradley Jr. and a more consistent hitter emerged.

The Sox also became more cognizant of the need to give their best players more days off. Throughout the season, the basis of

NEVER LOST MORE THAN 3 IN A ROW

many decisions was to make sure the players would have energy left for the postseason. The team was eliminated in the first round the previous two years.

"I am very proud of the way we have done things," Cora said. "I don't like talking about myself. I have a job to do, and one thing's for sure: I delegate. There are a lot of people who have done an outstanding job.

"When we put together a coaching staff, I wanted people I could trust. When the game starts at 7, I have no doubts the team will be prepared. They're ready to play."

The Sox lost on Opening Day at Tampa Bay, then won nine in a row.

They were 17-2 by late April, the talk of baseball.

The season could have taken a different turn on May 24, when the surprise decision was made to drop first baseman Hanley Ramirez from the roster. Cora decided Mitch Moreland would get more playing time and feared Ramirez could become a disruptive presence.

The Sox won five of the next six games, any controversy quickly pushed aside. After the rival Yankees challenged them in June, the Sox moved back into first place by themselves on July 2 and held that spot the rest of the season.

Through it all, the Sox never lost more than three games in a row.

"We turned the page — good, bad, or indifferent — from one day to the next," righthander Rick Porcello said. "That's what allowed us to maintain what we've been doing.

"When we needed it, Alex would talk to us. Everything he said to us was with a purpose. It wasn't something out of a book about leadership, it was genuine."

The Red Sox are not an underdog story. Their payroll is close to $235 million, approximately $28 million more than any other club.

They boosted payroll during the season, trading for righthander Nathan Eovaldi, second baseman Ian Kinsler, and first baseman Steve Pearce to fill needs.

But that did not guarantee success. The San Francisco Giants, Washington Nationals, and Los Angeles Angels all started the season with high payrolls and failed to make the playoffs.

The Sox made it work. Nobody roots for Goliath, but this team is undeniably likable.

"How can you not respect them?" Yankees manager Aaron Boone said. "They play the game the right way and they play hard. Alex did a great job with them."

Cora pushes back on such praise. He was a bench player for much of his career and still views the game through that prism.

"There's no Cora Magic," the manager said. "There are good players; there's a lot of talent. It takes a whole organization to be successful. That was the message from the get-go." ■

APR 8

After Mookie Betts ties the score on an RBI single, Andrew Benintendi (right) doubles Betts home (left) and caps Boston's 6-run rally in the bottom of the eighth inning for an 8-7 win over Tampa Bay. Boston improved to 8-1, the Rays fell to 1-8.

APR 1 1

The rivalry is renewed in ferocious fashion, after Boston reliever Joe Kelly hit the Yankees' Tyler Austin with a seventh-inning fastball — an unquestioned retaliation for Austin's hard slide into second base earlier in the game as Red Sox infielder Brock Holt attempted to turn a double play. A bench-clearing brawl and ejections ensue, and the "Joe Kelly Fight Club" T-shirt is born. Oh, the Sox lost the game, 10-7.

MAY 10

J.D. Martinez delivers his first important hit of the Sox-Yankees rivalry, a solo home run in the eighth inning that barely clears the right-field fence at the Stadium to snap a 4-4 tie and help Boston avert a sweep by the Yankees, who had won 17 of their previous 18 games, and rallied from a 4-0 deficit in the game.

JUNE 1

The Red Sox release Hanley Ramirez, one week after designating him for assignment. The team is responsible for the $15.25 million remaining on Ramirez's 2018 contract, but the move avoides Ramirez triggering a $22 million salary for 2019, based on at-bats. Ramirez, 34, hit just .163 with three homers and 12 RBIs in May. His best season in Boston was 2016, when he hit 30 homers with 111 RBIs while hitting .286.

JUNE 30

Chris Sale goes seven innings, allowing just one hit and fanning 11 Yankees to lead the Red Sox to an 11-0 win. Sale becames only the fifth pitcher since 1920 to pitch at least seven innings while allowing one hit or fewer, no runs, and at least 11 strikeouts. His performance is evocative of Pedro Martinez, who struck out 17 Yankees and gave up a single hit in a 3-1 win at New York in 1999. Rafael Devers goes 5-for-5 with a grand slam.

BY NICK CAFARDO • Globe Staff

You hear it around the league: The Red Sox play the game the right way.

They hit and run, steal bases, play defense, and pitch. Sounds like what's the big deal, who doesn't do that? Well, maybe some teams do it, but not as consistently as the Red Sox.

"They are one of the toughest teams to game-plan against," said Toronto bench coach DeMarlo Hale. "That's because they have several ways they can beat you. They're a disruptive team with their running game because they time their game so well. They create some problems for pitching staffs because they have such a high success rate with their steals. Just very sound all around."

Red Sox vice president — and Hall of Fame manager — Tony La Russa also commented on this in his first year observing the team. His clubs always were fundamentally sound, and even in this era of advanced analytics, in his mind the Red Sox haven't forgotten old-fashioned baseball.

You rarely see the Red Sox make a mental mistake. You might see physical errors from time to time, but few of any magnitude that cause games to be lost.

The Red Sox really have become that near-perfect hybrid, combining analytics with old-school scouting. Yes, they shift on defense, but their shifts have been effective.

"It's humbling to hear that," manager Alex Cora said. "I think we come to the park every day trying to play the game right, because if you don't beat yourself, that's half the battle. If you do things right, it kind of snowballs.

"You repeat success, you'll have success. I really believe that. So we try to play the game the right way every game. You can't be perfect all the time, but we just don't want to make a lot of mistakes."

David Price summed up the Red Sox this way: "We don't show anyone up. We come to play every day. We go first to third, we steal bases at a high percentage. We play defense. We run out every ball. We're kind of old school, but new school at the same time. We have a quiet kind of confidence before every game we play.

"I think our guys prepare as well as any team I've ever been on. There's a reason for everything we do, and when it's presented to us and there's proof to back up why we're doing something, it makes us all buy into it."

BASERUNNING

The Red Sox were first in stolen base percentage at 80.1 (125 for 156) and third in overall steals. A lot goes into that. First base coach Tom Goodwin is in charge of the running game. The Sox have been precise in timing pitchers and their time to the plate. They seem to hit it right. While they don't have speed

burners, they do have fast runners.

Pitcher Rick Porcello might be the fastest guy on the 25-man roster, but among positional players, Mookie Betts is the fastest. Xander Bogaerts, Andrew Benintendi, and Jackie Bradley Jr. all have above-average speed.

Statcast keeps a Sprint Speed category measured in feet per second. The average is 27 feet per second. A poor mark is 23 and an elite runner is 30.

Betts leads the Sox at 28.1 feet per second. Others: Bogaerts 27.9, Bradley 27.8, Benintendi 27.7, Eduardo Nunez 27.5, Rafael Devers 27.4, and Blake Swihart 27.2. The Red Sox have many above-average runners, and it shows not only in stolen bases but going from first to third and second to home.

And the Red Sox are smart. Last season they ran into a lot of outs, and that was happening again for the early part of 2018. But runners got smarter. They didn't take as many needless chances trying to force situations, and yet they remained aggressive.

"It's important to put pressure on the defense," Cora said. "I would never get upset about a player who did their best to take the extra base. As long as it made sense. And we're not perfect. There are times we take unnecessary chances, and when that happens, we have conversations about it."

DEFENSE

There was only one problem area on defense throughout the season and that was Devers at third base. His throwing was erratic, which can happen with young third basemen. Yankees rookie Miguel Andujar had similar problems.

The Red Sox were able to solidify their second base defense once they acquired Ian Kinsler. He's worked seamlessly with Bogaerts, who has become an above-average defensive shortstop. Cora doesn't pay attention to those who say otherwise about Bogaerts.

"We have our own defensive metrics and the way we measure our defense," Cora said. "Xander has done a tremendous job for us at his position."

In Baseball Reference's wins above average defensive measurements, the Red Sox rank second to the Houston Astros with 21.2, combining each position. Sox starting pitchers are fourth with 11.2, and their relievers are second at 3.8. The Sox rank first in right field, where their 8.2 is almost 5 points higher than the second-place Yankees.

Surprisingly, the Red Sox rank eighth in center field with 1.3, but they rank second in left field with 2.2. They rank No. 1 in overall outfield defense with 11.7.

The Red Sox rank last at third base with -2.6, 15th at first base with -0.6, 12th at shortstop with 1.6, last in catching with -3.4, and 29th at second base at -2.2.

The Red Sox clearly have the best defensive outfield in baseball. Your eyes tell you Betts has been the best right fielder and Bradley has been the best center fielder. The numbers tell you Benintendi has been the second-best left fielder.

PITCHING

The Red Sox used the third-fewest number of pitchers this season — 23, behind Colorado (21) and Houston (22), usually a good sign. They allowed 3.99 runs per game, tied for fifth fewest in baseball. They were eighth with a 3.75 team ERA and were fourth in strikeouts with 1,558.

They allowed 176 homers, ranking them 11th, and 512 walks, about middle of the pack.

The Red Sox have above-average pitching. It wasn't the best in baseball, but it was good enough to win 108 games. The prevailing theory has been that if you have above-average pitching, a great offense, and decent defense, your team will go far, and the Red Sox meet that criteria.

OFFENSE

The Red Sox lineup produced a major-league high 876 runs, 25 more than the Yankees. They hit 355 doubles, more than any other team in baseball, and 208 home runs (tied for eighth).

They had 829 RBIs (tops in baseball), 1,253 strikeouts (fifth fewest), and a .268 team average (9 points better than the second-best team, the Indians). They led the majors in on-base percentage (.339), slugging percentage (.453), and OPS (.792).

Interestingly, they had only seven sacrifice bunts all season.

This was the best offense in baseball. The first thing Cora did was flip the philosophy from the grind-it-out approach to the aggressive approach, which is what he had experienced in Houston the year before. The results were staggering.

Of course, adding J.D. Martinez was the biggest reason for the uptick from 2017. He had a great season and affected every player in the lineup because he acted as an extra hitting coach. The Red Sox truly missed David Ortiz, and when they didn't replace him in 2017, it showed. The 2017 Sox produced 785 runs, which was 10th overall. The difference of 91 runs proved immense. ■

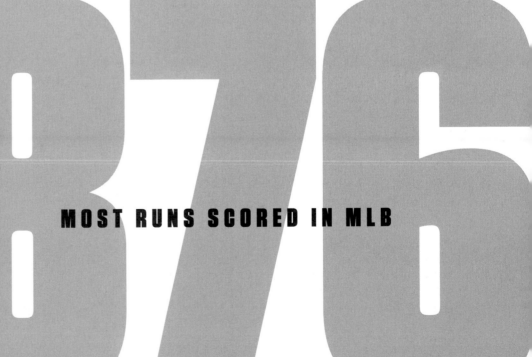

876
MOST RUNS SCORED IN MLB

JULY 2

Rick Porcello smiles toward the Red Sox dugout after he ripped a double off Max Scherzer of the Nationals, a former teammate and one of the best starting pitchers in baseball. Porcello's hit, which followed an intentional walk to Jackie Bradley Jr., brought home three runs for the Red Sox as they went on to a 4-3 victory over Washington.

Ace on base

RICK PORCELLO
has won the Cy Young Award and pitched in the World Series. But what he did on July 2 at Nationals Park in Washington, D.C., will rank with the best memories he takes away from his career.

Facing Max Scherzer, one of the best pitchers of his generation, Porcello launched a three-run double in the second inning. He also picked up the win as the Red Sox beat the Washington Nationals, 4-3. Oh, and he has a story he will tell the rest of his life.

"I've always said I love baseball because you never know what can happen," Porcello said. "I just wanted to put the ball in play."

Porcello and Scherzer played together in Detroit from 2010-14 and became close friends. Porcello was traded to the Red Sox after the 2014 season, about a month before Scherzer signed with the Nationals as a free agent. Until July 2, they had not faced each other.

Mitch Moreland singled to start the second inning. Brock Holt was hit by a pitch with one out before Scherzer struck out Sandy Leon on a wild pitch that advanced the runners. Nationals manager Dave Martinez intentionally walked Jackie Bradley Jr. to get to Porcello. Scherzer got ahead 0 and 2 with a slider and a cutter that Porcello swung through. Then he threw Porcello a 96.2-mile-per-hour fastball over the plate.

"He got to the top of his wind-up and I told myself, 'Start swinging,'" Porcello said. "Then, you know, I hit it." The ball sailed over the head of left fielder Juan Soto, who was understandably playing in.

"That was sick," fellow pitcher Eduardo Rodriguez said. "If I ever hit a double like that, I could strike out the rest of my career and still tell my kids I hit a three-run double off Scherzer." ■
PETER ABRAHAM

JULY 1 2

Mookie Betts celebrates with his teammates after producing one of the most thrilling at-bats of the season, working J.A. Happ (then pitching for Toronto) for 13 pitches and ripping a fourth-inning grand slam over the Monster to help extend the team's winning streak to 10 games with a 6-4 victory. It was the first major-league grand slam on an at-bat of 13 pitches or more since 1992. Boston improved to an MLB-best record of 66-29.

JULY 1 4

After failing to connect
on a grand slam in 2017,
the Red Sox mashed
10 of them in 2018, one
off the team record.
Xander Bogaerts hit
three of them, including
a walkoff blast to
straightaway center
field that beats Toronto,
6-2, in 10 innings and
prompts Bogaerts to
let out a howl as he
rounds the bases.

AUG 2

Steve Pearce rounds the bases after the second of his three homers over the Green Monster — in the third, fourth, and sixth innings — which accounted for six runs in a 15-7 blowout of the Yankees in the opener of a four-game series. Pearce becomes the sixth player to accomplish the three-HR feat in a Red Sox-Yankees game and the third Red Sox, joining Mo Vaughn (1997) and Kevin Millar (2004).

AUG 3

In his 297th career start, Rick Porcello puts together perhaps his most masterful outing, a complete-game one-hitter that required only 86 pitches. Porcello struck out nine Yankees and walked none, retiring 21 straight batters during one stretch of a 4-1 victory.

AUG 5

Just when the Yankees seem about to salvage the finale of a four-game series at Fenway, leading 4-1 in the ninth, Boston takes advantage of wildness by New York closer Aroldis Chapman to tie it. An RBI single by Andrew Benintendi (center) wins it in the 10th and the sweep pads Boston's lead to nine games, effectively ending the AL East race.

SEPT 5

The Red Sox score six runs in the top of the eighth inning, capped by a two-run single from pinch hitter Ian Kinsler, to tie the Braves in Atlanta, 7-7, only to fall behind by a run in the last of the eighth. Making his first start for the Sox after being called up in September, free-agent signee Brandon Phillips hits a two-run homer, then punctuates the blast that caps an improbable 9-8 Boston victory.

SEPT 1 2

Boston's outfield trio of Betts, Benintendi, and Bradley greet teammates after Boston's 100th victory. David Price (15-6) is brilliant for seven innings before the bullpen holds Toronto in check for a 1-0 win as the Red Sox reach 100 wins for the first time in 72 years.

SEPT 2 1

The Red Sox finally end the suspense and clinch the AL East title (below) with an 11-6 victory over the Yankees after two losses at the Stadium. Fittingly, Mookie Betts (left) puts it away with a towering three-run homer — his 30th — off Aroldis Chapman to cap a four-hit night. It was the third straight division title for Boston, which took over the division lead for good on July 2 and would end the season 108-54, a team record for victories.

106 WINS   106

ence

SEPT 2 4

Nathan Eovaldi allows
only one run in five
innings and four
relievers — with Matt
Barnes (32) finishing
up — complete a
6-2 victory over the
Orioles as the Red
Sox post their team-
record 106th win of
the season. The victory
eclipsed the 1912
Boston team, which
went 105-47 under
manager Jake Stahl
and defeated the
New York Giants
in the World Series.

SAMUEL DAMS   AMU

One for the record books

THEY HAD DOWNPLAYED IT

since the moment it was brought up, but there was nothing to downplay now. On Sept. 24, the 2018 Red Sox succeeded in winning the most games in franchise history.

"It's unreal," Red Sox manager Alex Cora said after a 6-2 victory over the Orioles at Fenway Park that set the club record for victories once held by the 1912 Red Sox. "You think about the history of the game and the history of this franchise, and to be a part of this ... I can't even explain it.

"It's a testament to the whole organization. ... We saw it in spring training when we had the best record in spring training and I know people kind of made fun of me for that, but it's not like I saw 106, but I saw a team that was very competitive, and they showed up every day."

Cora said he addressed the team after the game. He also said injured leader Dustin Pedroia, who has been with the Red Sox the longest and has won championships, spoke to the team as well.

Maybe the Red Sox didn't aspire to this record. Maybe they had their vision on other things. But if they don't appreciate it now, they will appreciate it when their careers are over and they realize, "We won that many games?"

Success is often luck. Success is often having a certain mojo at the right time. It can be a hot starting pitcher such as Madison Bumgarner in 2014 for the Giants. You just can't predict it. But one thing is for sure: When you win 106 games, it's more than luck. It's dominance. You could argue this Red Sox team benefited by the disparity of the haves and have-nots in baseball, which has reached a new high (or low). And it has nothing to do with money. The Oakland A's and Tampa Bay Rays are proof of that. The two teams with the lowest payrolls are surprising all of baseball.

Nevertheless, the Red Sox played the 2018 schedule better than anyone in baseball.

"People say we played the game the right way, and we did," Cora said. "We had our tough moments out there, but for the most part we did the little things and the big things to win games. When we couldn't hit the home runs, we won in other ways, and that's what good teams do.

"You don't have to win the same way to be successful. The more you can show that you win a game in different ways — maybe a well-pitched game, or a big offensive outburst, or a close game or an extra-inning game or a game when you have to use a lot of pitchers because your starter didn't have it that day. We won those games."

Maybe it wasn't a night for an all-out celebration, but at Cora's direction they took a moment to understand what they had done. And what they had done was pretty amazing. ∎

NICK CARARDO

Facts and
record-breaking

Figures

Dave Dombrowski, Red Sox president of baseball operations, takes a call as he converses with manager Alex Cora during spring training.

BY ALEX SPEIER • Globe Staff

The shift in the front office

Mookie Betts has a long list of highlights this year, but one stands out not for any act of brilliance on his part but for the fact that he hardly had to do anything.

On June 21, Twins first baseman Joe Mauer lined a ball to right-center field — ordinarily a hit or at least a ball that would have required a significant run to intercept it. But Betts stood in the path of the ball, barely moving in order to track it.

After he fired the ball back into the infield, Betts grinned at the dugout and pulled a card from his back pocket, waving it triumphantly. A new defensive alignment that had been suggested by the Red Sox analytics department — and printed on a small card for the outfielders to check — had been spot-on.

It was a moment that perhaps best captured the way information has been moved from the analytics department to the field, a change that speaks to the way manager Alex Cora altered the day-to-day functioning of the organization.

"Alex has put the stamp on, 'This is how we're going to do it,' " said Red Sox assistant general manager Eddie Romero. "He's kind of reformed the culture of how we're going to integrate data into decision-making."

The idea of Cora as someone who has "reformed the culture" of baseball operations flies in the face of a somewhat common (mis)perception. Last offseason, when several contending teams including the Red Sox replaced veteran managers with first-timers, many grumbled that a once-revered position had been reduced to a middle-manager.

According to such views, front offices weren't so much hiring authority figures as identifying someone who could do their bidding and serve as a conduit for data-driven analysis, all but filling out the lineup cards while offering managers a detailed script for how they were expected to handle a game.

"In my opinion, the role of manager has lessened in importance and the role of general manager and front-office guy has elevated," former manager Dusty Baker said earlier this year. "If [players] have a beef why they aren't playing, who do they talk to? Do they talk to the manager or the people pulling the strings for the manager? Some of the autonomy for the manager has been taken away, I think."

Such a view is likely an overstatement at best and simply wrong at worst. Certainly, in the case of the Red Sox and Cora, the manager is not merely a reflection of the baseball operations department but an agent of change within it. Perhaps most notably, Cora has been an agent of change for the Red Sox regarding information and analytics, the areas most often caricatured as corrosive to the modern manager. He has been a catalyst for the increased integration of data into the team's preparation and game management, pushing the envelope beyond even what the front office expected.

Such a development was part of the allure of hiring Cora after his year as bench coach for the 2017 World Series champion Houston Astros. In the words of Boston president of baseball operations Dave Dombrowski, a manager's potential application of analytics was "a large part of our interview process."

Though the Red Sox had once been at the vanguard of data and analytics, they recognized that other organizations (notably the Astros) had surpassed them. The Sox committed considerable resources to closing the gap in recent years, hiring several analysts and building more robust systems to handle the explosion of information.

Such additions affected roster moves and pitching instruction, but the analytics department wasn't much involved with in-game management. When the Sox interviewed Cora, Brad Ausmus, and Ron Gardenhire as potential replacements for John Farrell last October, they hoped to gain insight into how each candidate viewed the role of analytics in running a game.

Cora already was clear-eyed about how to integrate the work of the analytics department into roster management based on his year with Houston.

"He was often talking directly to me about these things during the interview," said Red Sox vice president of baseball research and development Zack Scott. "I didn't go into it with any idea that we'd be tightly integrated with what we were doing on a daily basis. He kind of changed that.

"I came away from that process thinking, 'Wow, he's really invested in this stuff. He's really all-in.' " ∎

BY DAN SHAUGHNESSY • Globe Staff

rookie of the year

Alex Cora

might be Boston's best "rookie" since Fred Lynn in 1975 or Larry Bird in '79. It wasn't like this for Bill Belichick in Year 1. The Hoodie went 5-11 in his first year as head coach of the Patriots. Red Auerbach? In 1950-51, Auerbach got the Celtics over .500, but they were swept in the first round of the playoffs. Brad Stevens?

He didn't make the playoffs in his first season on the bench.

Cora had the second-most successful rookie year of managing in the history of Major League Baseball, winning a whopping 108 regular-season games. Only Ralph Houk (109-53 with the 1961 Yankees) won more games than Cora in his first season and Houk had Roger Maris, Mickey Mantle, Yogi Berra, and Whitey Ford. Cora has a pretty good roster, too, but nothing like the '61 Yanks.

The 42-year-old field boss of the Local Nine has been everybody's favorite since Day 1. Players, owners, team staffers, and media members all love him. And fans have spared him the slings and arrows traditionally aimed at any man who sits on the hot seat on the street formerly known as Yawkey Way.

The only grumbling came when Cora would stick to his plan of "resting" players even when it appeared he could win a game if he just bent his own rules slightly.

This happened Opening Day in Tampa when Cora told Craig Kimbrel he wouldn't be pitching, then left Kimbrel on the shelf while the Sox were blowing a 4-0 lead to the Rays in the eighth inning. Cora patiently watched Joe Kelly put a match to the lead in a hideous loss, triggering one wise guy to write, "Bring back John Farrell."

It was Cora's worst day of the season, but it was a fair measure of the Cora Way. And more often than not, it has worked. At a record pace.

While the 2018 Red Sox stacked wins like cordwood, Cora stuck to his system. Mookie Betts would get a day off when Cora could have used Mookie as a late-game pinch-hitter. Ditto for J.D. Martinez. Even if there was a scheduled off day the following day, Cora never wavered.

In this sprint we've had some grumbling in the final days of the magical 2018 season. After the Red Sox clinched home-field advantage throughout the playoffs, the manager treated the rest of the schedule with the same urgency you'd expect him to have in Fort Myers.

Everything was about getting ready for the playoffs. Even if it meant losing to the Yankees. No starting pitcher worked more than five innings. Every position player had at least two days off.

This resulted in a mini-slump at the end of the season. The Sox lost three straight, five of seven, seven of 11.

Cora was teasingly asked if Game No. 162 — the season finale against the hated Yankees — was a "must-win" game.

"Nah," he said seriously.

Would you rather finish on a winning note than go into the playoffs on a four-game losing streak, we wondered?

"If we go in with an eight-, nine-game winning streak people would be saying it doesn't matter," said the manager. "We've been planning this for a while. After we clinched we've been taking care of the pitching staff."

In some ways, this was mildly reminiscent of the final days of the 2016 season when the Red Sox lost five of their last six while honoring David Ortiz every night. Then they got swept in three by the Indians. It amounted to eight losses and six Ortiz celebrations over the last nine games.

The Cora Men righted the ship, thrashing the New Yorkers, 10-2, in the season finale. So there was no four-game losing streak hanging around until the playoffs started.

"We're happy with that, but we know what's coming," the rookie manager said after the game. "The goal is to win 11 games in October." ■

BY PETER ABRAHAM • Globe Staff

face of the franchise

He hits for power, steals bases, and plays the expansive right field at Fenway Park better than anybody since Dwight Evans. At 25,

Mookie Betts

is one of the best all-around players in baseball and that should be enough.

It's not, of course. Betts also is supposed to be a clubhouse leader, especially during those times when the passion that can make playing in Boston such a thrill becomes a burden.

Nobody asks to be the face of their franchise, it just happens.

"I think it's one of those myths, that somebody who is a good player should be a leader," Betts said. "People take it as a bad thing if you're not a leader. But there's nothing wrong with that. It's one of those things that can take time to develop."

As the Red Sox prepared to start the 2018 season, Betts understood that more is expected of him. It's something he has discussed with manager Alex Cora at length.

That transition started last season and in retrospect, Betts wasn't ready for it.

Betts finished second to Mike Trout for American League MVP in 2016 and expectations were for him to repeat that performance, if not improve on it. But when David Ortiz retired, opposing teams were able to pitch more carefully to Betts.

"You always look at a lineup and pick out the player you don't want to have beat you," Yankees pitcher CC Sabathia said. "That was Papi for a long time. Then it became Mookie."

The lineup changed further on April 21 when Baltimore's Manny Machado slid aggressively into Dustin Pedroia, badly injuring the second baseman's left knee. Pedroia played in only 89 of the remaining 145 games.

With Ortiz off starting a new life and Pedroia diminished, even more attention shifted to Betts, who was in just his third full season.

Betts, Xander Bogaerts, Jackie Bradley Jr., and the other young players on the team were left carrying a heavier load on the field and off.

"One of the biggest challenges in clubhouse dynamics is when young players are growing," Red Sox president of baseball operations Dave Dombrowski said. "It was a growing process for us last year and there were times we struggled with it. It can be hard to find leaders."

The Sox were successful in the standings, winning the AL East by two games. But the atmosphere around the team was often joyless.

"Looking back on it, we didn't really have as much fun with it as we should have," Betts said.

In January, Cora had a lengthy conversation with Betts that centered on leadership. It's a theme they've touched on several times since.

"I don't want him to get out of his comfort zone and be somebody people want him to be," Cora said. "Take care of your business first."

The Sox work with their players on personal development and have expanded their staff to include four mental skills coordinators. Leadership strategies can be taught, but that doesn't always mean they'll be used.

"It's not in everybody's DNA," Dombrowski said.

"There are Hall of Fame players who weren't necessarily leaders. But we have programs in place to assist that."

The players don't see leadership as an outsider might, Bradley said. It's not making a speech or some public display of emotion. It's usually something less obvious.

"You can lead by example, you can lead with your voice, some people lead by their strength or their sense of humor," Bradley said. "It's not necessarily directing people. It's taking your strength and using it to your advantage. A lot of different qualities go into being a leader. Mookie has those qualities. How he uses those is up to him." ▪

BY ALEX SPEIER • Globe Staff

samurai of swing

It isn't supposed to work this way. Players aren't supposed to hit with power the way Red Sox slugger

J.D. Martinez

does.

So how does Martinez do it? How does he take pitches that would jam other hitters and drive them 350 feet?

"You got an hour?" Martinez smirked when asked to describe his swing path.

Perhaps the most telling part of Martinez's swing is that the efforts to describe it draw not necessarily from baseball but from far-flung realms — among them another sport, amusement park rides, and ancient Japanese traditions.

For most of his baseball life, Martinez's swing was intended to travel a straight line. He was in the hands-to-the-ball school, trying to take a direct path with his bat to a pitch — and swinging down to the point of impact, in a way that often yielded liners or, more disappointingly, ground balls. He was failing to take advantage of his long arms and natural strength that offered the raw ingredients of a power hitter.

After the 2013 season, Martinez engaged in a radical overhaul of his swing under the guidance of hitting instructors Craig Wallenbrock and Robert Van Scoyoc.

"He's a guy who built his swing," said Red Sox hitting coach Tim Hyers. "He kind of changed everything around."

The direct line to the ball is now a distant memory. Instead, Martinez sets his swing in motion with the barrel of the bat moving in an almost circular path to and through the ball that one evaluator described as "a Ferris wheel."

During the downswing, Martinez keeps his hips and shoulders closed while whipping the bat down with his arms. Rather than sending the bat in a line toward where he thinks the ball will be, on his downswing, Martinez is trying to "groove his swing in a certain lane" close to his body, according to Red Sox assistant hitting coach Andy Barkett.

The bat remains in a neutral position in the downswing, as does Martinez's body. His shoulders, hips, and legs are all aligned with the barrel of the bat. To Wallenbrock, that starting point is crucial to permitting a hitter to attack a wide variety of pitches.

"Never commit the barrel," said Wallenbrock. "I liken it to the samurai sword. The samurai warrior is told to never lose your blade. If you lose your blade, you can only fight one warrior at a time. If you hold your blade, you can fight multiple warriors because you're going through and not to your opponent."

In perhaps more familiar terms,

Hyers likens the movement of Martinez's bat to that of a golfer who remains square to the ball.

"He's not a spinner," said Hyers. "He's a guy who stays in his legs and has really good direction. What I mean by that is he has a good foundation with his hips underneath him. It allows his hands to work through [the swing]."

That downswing is what positions Martinez, on his upswing, to attack the pitch across the broadest possible expanse of the strike zone. By the time he's ready to send the barrel through the strike zone, it's moving up and "on plane," matching the trajectory of the pitch.

The notion of an uppercut, on-plane swing – famously espoused by Ted Williams – resonates with Martinez.

"I've always thought about numbers," said Martinez. "I've always been good at math. (A swing is) kind of just angle-matching. I try to match the plane the pitch is on. I'm not a ball-hitter. I'm a plane-matcher."

Yet even as an uppercut swing through contact has become the new norm in baseball, Martinez still represents a distinctive practitioner of the art. His barrel enters the strike zone on its upward trajectory deeper in the strike zone than most.

"His length in his swing path is so much longer than a lot of guys who hit in this league," said Hyers.

"He's got such good hand-eye coordination and such masterful body control. There's not many people who can do it, but he can. There's only one J.D. Martinez," said Barkett. ■

BY PETER ABRAHAM • Globe Staff

power hitter unleashed

Xander Bogaerts

was doing just fine playing by the rules others set for him. He made his major league debut in 2013 at age 20, helped win a World Series that season, and was an All-Star three years after that.

In his first two years of arbitration, Bogaerts came away with $11.5 million. He had no complaints.

The Red Sox shortstop was a predictable and productive hitter. He would almost always take the first pitch and with runners on base cut down on his swing and poke the ball the other way to right field.

"I was good at finding that hole," Bogaerts said.

He was. Bogaerts hit .283 with a .750 OPS in his first four full seasons and averaged 70 RBIs. Were it not for a hand injury in the second half of the 2017 season, those statistics would be even better.

At 25, Bogaerts gave all that up this season. The safe and predictable player took another path.

When Bogaerts drove in four runs in a September game, he did more than reach 100 RBIs for the first time in his career. He also showed how much he had changed his approach.

With teammate J.D. Martinez on first base in the sixth inning, Bogaerts worked the count full against reliever Cody Carroll. In past years, Bogaerts would have looked at the hole on the right side. He instead loaded up, kept his hands back, and launched a fastball over the wall in center field. Those two RBIs gave him 100.

That teammate Eduardo Rodriguez had told him to hit a home run before he left the dugout was in Bogaerts's head the whole time.

"I kept hearing that voice," he said. "So why not?"

His at-bat in the first inning was even more of a departure.

With runners on second and third and one out, Bogaerts got ahead in the count, 3 and 0. None of the pitches from rookie Ryan Meisinger were close to the plate.

From the time he signed with the Sox in 2009, Bogaerts had been taught to take that pitch, work the count, and grind the starter down.

But this time, Bogaerts swung at an inside fastball and pulled it down the line into the left field corner. Two runs scored.

It was just the fifth time in his career Bogaerts swung at a 3-0 pitch and the second time he had a hit.

"We were very happy with that one," manager Alex Cora said.

Cora, who played for the Red Sox, understood the organization's philosophy. But he also grasped how baseball has changed in recent seasons. Bullpens are now loaded with hard-throwing pitchers who also have a breaking ball, and it's not necessarily an advantage to wait the starter out.

Cora didn't order Bogaerts to change his approach when they sat down before the season. He instead explained what he saw in 2017 as the bench coach of the Houston Astros. In Bogaerts, Cora saw a talented player capable of more but bound by what was expected of him.

"This guy, he's better [than that]. He can do some damage early on in the count," Cora said. "When I got the job [with the Red Sox] I said, 'This is what people see from you guys.' Some of them were surprised. They had no idea. It was part of the culture."

Bogaerts is especially proud of reaching 100 RBIs, something no Red Sox shortstop had done since Nomar Garciaparra in 2003.

"I never envisioned it," Bogaerts said. "But I wanted it."

Bogaerts has hit fourth or fifth all but 24 times this season, usually behind Martinez. Cora wanted him in RBI situations knowing Martinez would have a high on-base percentage. The manager also told Bogaerts to forget his programming and look for pitches he could lay into.

"He really bought into what we wanted him to do as a hitter, try to drive the ball, do some damage," Cora said. "He's taken advantage of it."

Bogaerts is now part of the conversation when discussing the best shortstops in the game.

"He understands how talented he is," Cora said. "He just doesn't express it. But I do. I'm very proud of my shortstop." ∎

BY CHAD FINN • Globe Staff

legend in the making?

I can't swear to you there will never be another Pedro Martinez. The original himself was pretty close to implausible. The original was undersized and unimposing, until he stepped up those six inches to the top of a pitcher's mound. It was there, in his workspace, where everything about him became larger than life: his talent, of course, but also his competitiveness, his charisma, even, when the game was done, his candor.

It's tempting to suggest that no one should be compared to Pedro, given that if anyone is beyond compare it should be a pitcher who, in seven years with the Red Sox, went 117-37 (80 games over .500!) with a 2.52 ERA and 190 adjusted ERA during the cheating heart of the performance-enhancing drug era. Roger Clemens? Pedro has everything over him but longevity, including a better grasp of the English language.

So let's go with this: From purely a baseball perspective, the closest thing the Red Sox have had to Pedro — in effectiveness if not aesthetics

— is the lanky lefty they acquired in a trade with the Chicago White Sox.

Before he injured his shoulder, Sale's best performance was the 50th of his Red Sox career and it came against the Yankees June 30. He held the host Yankees to one hit and one walk over seven shutout innings, striking out 11 in an 11-1 win. Per Bill James's Game Score, it was his best start of this season, the fourth-best of his Red Sox career, and tied for ninth-best in his nine-year career.

In that venue against that lineup, it was a fine feat, and not an unfamiliar one.

Sale's first 50 starts stack up to other prominent Red Sox pitchers over the last 40 years. He had nine fewer wins than Pedro over that stretch, and Pedro had the lower ERA in a hitter-happy time when pretty much no one other than him had a low ERA. But Sale's WHIP, K/9, and K/BB rates were better. He's not Pedro. But he's done a lot of

Pedro-like things, and only legends and aspiring legends can say that.

The main difference, and one I hope is bridged, is in their public personalities. Pedro was an open book. Sale often just shows us the dust jacket. He's accountable and quick to credit teammates, and his humility seems authentic. But he's also low-key when there are clues that his private personality is not low-key at all, and in a wholly likable way. He's not a superstar mystery in the Kevin Garnett sense, but you do get the sense the public would love his private persona.

When the Red Sox acquired him from the White Sox in December 2016, we knew he was a cut-up in one sense — wielding scissors and his own rage, he famously turned ill-fitting White Sox throwback jerseys into throwback shreds of useless fabric one time.

But who knew he was a cut-up when it came to having a good time? If you saw the picture of Sale and his Red Sox teammates boarding the team plane in Washington in full Fourth of July regalia, you must have done a double-take before the inevitable burst of laughter.

There was Sale, the supposedly straight-laced ace, wearing a bow tie, cutoff jorts, and a bucket hat. What he was not wearing was a shirt. I'm not sure we needed to see the front of Sale. But it was amusing to see that side from him. Perhaps he'll reveal more of it off the field once he and the Red Sox fully achieve what they want to on it. ◼

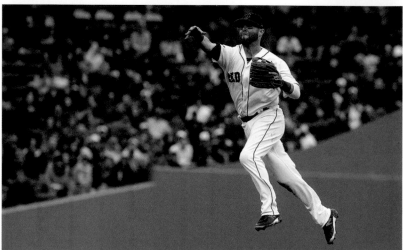

Pedey as mentor

For the first time since 2005, **Dustin Pedroia** was not on the field when the Red Sox played in the postseason. But the second baseman, who spent most of the season on the disabled list recovering from knee surgery, still had a role.

Manager Alex Cora wanted the 35-year-old Pedroia around the team to share his insights and provide advice to players when asked. Pedroia worked with Rafael Devers on infield fundamentals and talked to Ian Kinsler about his slump at the plate.

"He's a more mature guy," Cora said. "He's a leader in the clubhouse. I walk into the [batting] cage for whatever reason, and he's there talking to somebody.

"It's a different role for him ... but he's been great. His energy is still there. I know he's dying to go out there and perform. But he's been a great teammate. We're very proud of him. He's not a distraction."

Cora and Pedroia were teammates from 2005 to '08 and became close friends. Cora sees a change in Pedroia's demeanor now.

"Compared to when I played with him, he's not the loud guy: 'I'm the Laser Show, rah, rah.' He's a lot different," Cora said. "He'll come to the office, and we talk about the team.

"He cares. He cares a lot about this organization. He loves the fact that we're in this situation. I wanted him to be here. I told him, 'You're going to contribute regardless, on the field or off the field.' He's doing it in the clubhouse."

Pedroia was in Arizona doing rehab work for much of the summer and returned to the team in September. He has kept a low profile with the media and when the team celebrated its division title.

"Just enjoying it," he said. "It's been easier that the team is so good. It's fun to watch."

With Pedroia able to play in only

Pedroia encourages catcher Christian Vazquez (top left), tosses to first in one of his few games in 2018, holds court in the dugout pre-game and pitches to his son, Cole, in spring training.

three games this season, the Red Sox were 14th in the American League with a .658 OPS at second base and last with only eight home runs. The Sox were seventh in the league with a .758 OPS in 2017. Pedroia hit .293 with a .760 OPS last season.

Pedroia has played in 51 postseason games. Only David Ortiz (76) and Jason Varitek (63) have more with the Sox. ■

PETER ABRAHAM

6011
AT BATS SINCE 2006

Boston Red Sox

POSITION PLAYERS

BENINTENDI
Andrew
HR 16
RBI 87
BA .290
2Bs 41

Top 20 in AL in runs, on-base, RBIs, walks

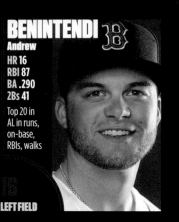

16
LEFT FIELD

BETTS
Mookie
HR 32
RBI 80
BA .346
SB 30

First to win batting title in 30-HR, 30-SB year

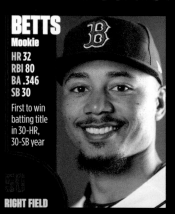

50
RIGHT FIELD

BOGAERTS
Xander
HR 23
RBI 103
BA .288
2Bs 45

Fifth in AL in RBIs, led MLB with 3 grand slams

2
SHORTSTOP

BRADLEY JR.
Jackie
HR 13
RBI 59
BA .234
2Bs 33

Team was 36-3 when he had at least one RBI

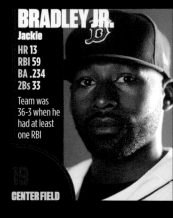

19
CENTER FIELD

DEVERS
Rafael
HR 21
RBI 66
BA .240
2Bs 24

3rd Sox player to hit 20 HRs before age 22

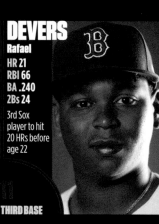

11
THIRD BASE

HOLT
Brock
HR 7
RBI 46
BA .277
2Bs 18

Went 5-for-13 as pinch hitter with 2 HRs

12
UTILITY PLAYER

KINSLER
Ian
HR 1
RBI 16
BA .242
ABs 132

Hit .289 over final 50 games of season

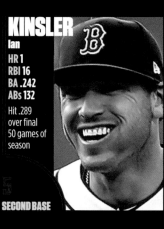

5
SECOND BASE

LEON
Sandy
HR 5
RBI 22
BA .177
2Bs 12

Led MLB with 3.29 catcher's ERA in 89 games

3
CATCHER

MARTINEZ
J.D.
HR 43
RBI 130
BA .330
2Bs 37

Led MLB with 130 RBI and 358 total bases

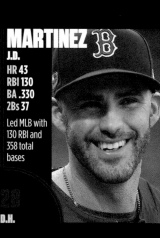

28
D.H.

MORELAND
Mitch
HR 15
RBI 68
BA .245
2Bs 23

Career highs in games, runs, 2Bs, and walks

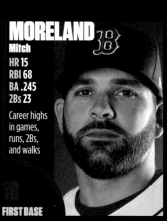

18
FIRST BASE

NUNEZ
Eduardo
HR 10
RBI 44
BA .265
2Bs 23

Batted .297 in his final 42 games of the season

36
THIRD BASE

PEARCE
Steve
HR 7
RBI 26
BA .279
2Bs 8

Hit .368 with runners in scoring position

25
FIRST BASE

RAMIREZ
Hanley
HR 4
RBI 10
BA .216
ABs 177

Hitless in final 21 ABs, released on June 1

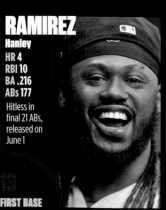

13
FIRST BASE

SWIHART
Blake
HR 3
RBI 18
BA .229
2Bs 10

Played six positions: C, 1B, 2B, 3B, LF, RF

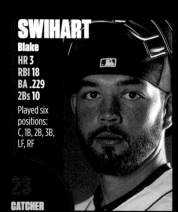

23
CATCHER

VAZQUEZ
Christian
HR 3
RBI 16
BA .207
2Bs 10

34 pct. caught-stealing leads active Cs

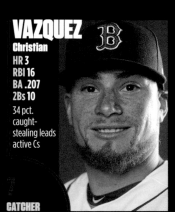

7
CATCHER

EXTENDED ROSTER

PITCHER	W-L	ERA	Inn	App	GS
D. POMERANZ	2-6	6.08	74.0	26	11
S. WRIGHT	3-1	2.68	53.2	20	4
T. THORNBURG	2-0	5.63	24.0	25	0
B. POYNER	1-0	3.22	22.1	20	0
W. CUEVAS	0-2	7.41	17.0	9	1

PLAYER	BA	HR	RBI	G	AB
T. LIN	.246	1	6	37	65
S. TRAVIS	.222	1	7	19	36
B. PHILLIPS	.130	1	2	9	23
D. PEDROIA	.091	0	0	3	11

2018 Roster

PITCHERS

BARNES
Matt
W-L 6-4
ERA 3.65
App 62
Inn 61.2

Averaged 14 Ks per 9 IP ; opponents hit .204

THROWS RIGHT

BRASIER
Ryan
W-L 2-0
ERA 1.60
App 34
Inn 33.2

Allowed only 2 walks over final 24 appearances

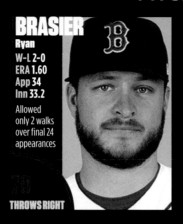

THROWS RIGHT

EOVALDI
Nathan
W-L 3-3
ERA 3.33
App 12
Inn 54

Only 1 ER allowed in 23 IP vs. Yankees in 2018

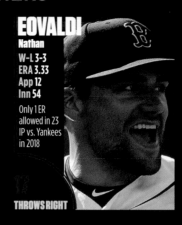

THROWS RIGHT

HEMBREE
Heath
W-L 4-1
ERA 4.20
App 67
Inn 60.0

Allowed only 1 hit in 10.2 innings in June

THROWS RIGHT

JOHNSON
Brian
W-L 4-5
ERA 4.17
App 38
Inn 99.1

Went 3-0 in five starts in August

THROWS LEFT

KELLY
Joe
W-L 4-2
ERA 4.39
App 73
Inn 65.2

His 73 games most for Boston since 2013 (Uehara)

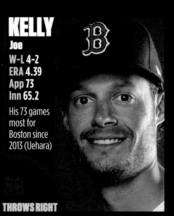

THROWS RIGHT

KIMBREL
Craig
W-L 5-1
ERA 2.74
Svs 42
Inn 62.1

42 saves were tied for 2nd-most in Boston

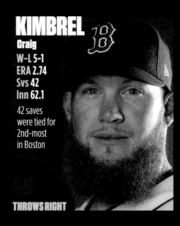

THROWS RIGHT

PORCELLO
Rick
W-L 17-7
ERA 4.28
GS 33
Inn 191.1

Struck out career-high 191 (8.94 per 9 inn.)

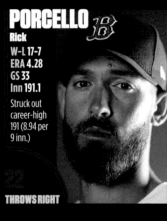

THROWS RIGHT

PRICE
David
W-L 16-7
ERA 3.58
GS 30
Inn 176.0

Was 6-1 with 2.25 ERA in final 11 starts

THROWS LEFT

RODRIGUEZ
Eduardo
W-L 13-5
ERA 3.82
App 27
Inn 129.2

Career-high 24-inning scoreless streak

THROWS LEFT

SALE
Chris
W-L 12-4
ERA 2.11
GS 24
Inn 158

Had longest scoreless streak in MLB (34 innings).

THROWS LEFT

VELAZQUEZ
Hector
W-L 7-2
ERA 3.18
App 47
Inn 85

Was 6-0 with a 2.66 ERA before All-Star break

THROWS RIGHT

WORKMAN
Brandon
W-L 6-1
ERA 3.27
App 43
Inn 64.2

Went 3-0 with a 1.96 ERA in 22 home games

THROWS RIGHT

'Everybody's on board. Everybody knows that they have a role, and they can contribute. Regardless if you're starting, you have to pay attention to the game.' ALEX CORA

CORA
Alex
Age 42
W-L 108-54

His 108 wins 2nd-most for a first-year manager (Houk, NYY, 1961)

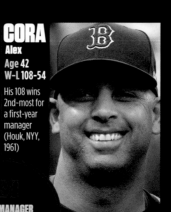

MANAGER

COACHES

RON ROENICKE | Bench coach

TIM HYERS | Hitting coach

ANDY BARKETT | Assistant hitting coach

DANA LEVANGIE | Pitching coach

TOM GOODWIN | First base coach

CARLOS FEBLES | Third base coach

CRAIG BJORNSON | Bullpen coach

2018 REGULAR SEASON

DATE	OPPONENT	SCORE		PLACE			THE LOWDOWN
MARCH/APRIL							
3/29	@ Tampa Bay	L	4-6	4th	—	1	Span triples with bases loaded in the 8th.
3/30	@ Tampa Bay	W	1-0	3rd	—	1	Price pitches seven shutout innings in season debut.
3/31	@ Tampa Bay	W	3-2	1st	T		Bogaerts homers, Porcello allows one run in 5 1/3 IP.
4/1	@ Tampa Bay	W	2-1	1st	♠	1	Devers' RBI double in 6th helps Velazquez earn first win.
4/2	@ Miami	W	7-3	1st	♠	1	Betts and Ramirez hit first HRs of the season.
4/3	@ Miami	W	4-2	1st	♠	1	Ramirez hits two-run double with two outs in 13th inning.
4/5	Tampa Bay	W	3-2	1st	♠	2	Ramirez hits bases-loaded single in the 12th for the walk-off win.
4/7	Tampa Bay	W	10-3	1st	♠	2.5	Bogaerts hits a grand slam and has career-high six RBIs.
4/8	Tampa Bay	W	8-7	1st	♠	2.5	Benintendi hits tie-breaking double in a six-run 8th inning.
4/10	New York Yankees	W	14-1	1st	♠	2	Betts goes 4-5 with a grand slam for ninth win in a row.
4/11	New York Yankees	L	7-10	1st	♠	2	Tyler Austin rushes mound after being hit by a pitch from Joe Kelly.
4/12	New York Yankees	W	6-3	1st	♠	2.5	Porcello strikes out six in seven scoreless innings.
4/13	Baltimore	W	7-3	1st	♠	2.5	Rodriguez strikes out eight batters, Nunez hits three-run HR.
4/14	Baltimore	W	10-3	1st	♠	3	Offense shines, Sox off to best start in team history (118 years).
4/15	Baltimore	W	3-1	1st	♠	3.5	Benintendi goes 3-4 with a RBI, Sale dominant.
4/17	@ Los Angeles Angels	W	10-1	1st	♠	3	Betts homers three times.
4/18	@ Los Angeles Angels	W	9-0	1st	♠	3	Devers hits first career grand slam.
4/19	@ Los Angeles Angels	W	8-2	1st	♠	4	Betts hits second leadoff homer in three games
4/20	@ Oakland	W	7-3	1st	♠	4	Moreland hits grand slam, Sox improve to 17-2.
4/21	@ Oakland	L	0-3	1st	♠	4	Sean Manaea pitches first no-hitter against Red Sox in 25 years.
4/22	@ Oakland	L	1-4	1st	♠	4	Khris Davis hits three-run HR off Price in the 8th.
4/24	@ Toronto	L	3-4	1st	♠	3	Granderson hits walk-off HR in 10th inning.
4/25	@ Toronto	W	4-3	1st	♠	4	Betts homers twice to snap three-game losing streak.
4/26	@ Toronto	W	5-4	1st	♠	4	Martinez homers and drives in three.
4/27	Tampa Bay	L	3-4	1st	♠	3	Blake Snell (nine Ks) outpitches Pomeranz.
4/28	Tampa Bay	L	6-12	1st	♠	2	Span hits inside-the-park HR, Price and Johnson both allow 5 ER.
4/29	Tampa Bay	W	4-3	1st	♠	2	Leon hits RBI single in 8th to seal the win.
4/30	Kansas City	W	10-6	1st	♠	3	Bogaerts hits grand slam, Sox finish April with most wins ever.
MAY							
5/1	Kansas City	L	6-7	1st	♠	2	Kimbrel blows the save, Soler hits three-run HR in the 13th.
5/2	Kansas City	W	5-4	1st	♠	2	Betts hits three homers for second time in eight days.
5/3	@ Texas	L	5-11	1st	♠	1	Mazara totals 5 RBIs in Price's third loss in a row.
5/4	@ Texas	W	5-1	1st	♠	1	Porcello dominates Blue Jays (6 IP, 1 ER, 8 Ks).
5/5	@ Texas	W	6-5	1st	♠	1	Sox rally to take lead in the ninth, Kimbrel gets 300th career save.
5/6	@ Texas	W	6-1	1st	♠	1	Sale strikes out 12 in dominant effort.
5/8	@New York Yankees	L	2-3	1st	T		Stanton homers twice off Pomeranz.
5/9	@New York Yankees	L	6-9	2nd	▼	1	Porcello struggles, Sox fall to second place.
5/10	@New York Yankees	W	5-4	1st	T		J.D. Martinez hits go-ahead HR in the 8th.
5/11	@Toronto	L	3-5	1st	T		Maile homers twice in walk-off win.
5/12	@Toronto	W	5-2	1st	T		Ramirez hits third HR in four games as Price returns from sore wrist.
5/13	@Toronto	W	5-3	1st	T		Betts makes amazing diving play to save the game.
5/14	Oakland	L	5-6	2nd	▼	.5	Manaea beats Sox again behind three A's home runs.
5/15	Oakland	L	3-5	2nd	▼	.5	Mengden outpitches Rodriguez.
5/16	Oakland	W	6-4	1st	T		Sale strikes out nine as Sox avoid first sweep of season.
5/17	Baltimore	W	6-2	1st	♠	.5	Price pitches first complete game of the season (2 ER, 9 Ks).
5/18	Baltimore	L	4-7	1st	♠	.5	Cobb (6 1/3 IP, 3 ER) earns first victory as an Oriole.
5/19	Baltimore	W	6-3	1st	♠	.5	Betts and Benintendi hit back-to-back HRs.
5/20	Baltimore	W	5-0	1st	♠	.5	Martinez has first multi-HR game with Boston.
5/22	@ Tampa Bay	W	4-2	1st	♠	1	Betts hits league-leading 16th home run.
5/23	@ Tampa Bay	W	4-1	1st	♠	2	Sox bats struggle vs. Blake Snell, again.
5/24	@ Tampa Bay	L	3-6	1st	♠	1.5	Reynolds, Stubbs each collect three RBIs on three hits.
5/25	Atlanta	W	6-2	1st	♠	1.5	Betts and Martinez each homer; Ramirez designated for assignment.
5/26	Atlanta	W	8-6	1st	♠	2.5	Atlanta unable to capitalize on early Pomeranz exit.
5/27	Atlanta	L	1-7	1st	♠	1.5	Sale gives up six runs in 4 1/3 innings.

DATE	OPPONENT	SCORE	PLACE			THE LOWDOWN
5/28	Toronto	W 8-3	1st	▲	2.5	Sox bats dominate Sanchez.
5/29	Toronto	W 8-3	1st	▲	2.5	Leon (HR, 2 2B) powers eight-run game for the Sox.
5/30	Toronto	W 6-4	1st	▲	2.5	Martinez hits HR to complete the series sweep.
5/31	@ Houston	L 2-4	1st	▲	2	Correa snaps 0-10 streak with a two-run HR.

JUNE

DATE	OPPONENT	SCORE	PLACE			THE LOWDOWN
6/1	@ Houston	L 3-7	1st	▲	1	Houston's bullpen pitches five scoreless innings.
6/2	@ Houston	W 5-4	1st	▲	1	Vazquez and Benintendi homer in a three-run 7th inning.
6/3	@ Houston	W 9-3	1st	▲	1.5	Benintendi homers for second game in a row.
6/5	Detroit	W 6-0	1st	▲	1.5	Wright pitches seven scoreless innings in first start of season.
6/6	Detroit	W 7-1	1st	▲	1.5	Benintendi hits third HR in four games.
6/7	Detroit	L 2-7	1st	▲	1	Tigers score five runs in 1st inning off Beeks in first career start.
6/8	Chicago White Sox	L 0-1	1st	T		Sox manage just three hits for the game.
6/9	Chicago White Sox	W 4-2	1st	T		Martinez blasts 21st HR of the season.
6/10	Chicago White Sox	L 2-5	1st	T		Late error by Bogaerts seals it for Chicago.
6/11	@ Baltimore	W 2-0	1st	▲	.5	Holt and Bradley win with sacrifice flies in the 12th.
6/12	@ Baltimore	W 6-4	1st	▲	.5	Eduardo Rodriguez wins fifth straight start.
6/13	@ Baltimore	W 5-1	1st	▲	1.5	Sale ejected in 7th, Boston completes the sweep.
6/14	@ Seattle	W 2-1	1st	▲	1.5	Bogaerts breaks tie with HR in the sixth.
6/15	@ Seattle	L 6-7	1st	▲	.5	Span hits pinch-hit double in 8th.
6/16	@ Seattle	L 0-1	2nd	▼	.5	LeBlanc (0 ER, 9 Ks) dominates in 7 2/3 innings.
6/17	@ Seattle	W 9-3	1st	▲	.5	Devers, Bradley, and Bogaerts homer in rout.
6/19	@ Minnesota	L 2-6	2nd	▼	1	Twins score 4 off Sox bullpen.
6/20	@ Minnesota	L 1-4	2nd	▼	2	Lynn tosses five scoreless as Twins allow 0 earned runs.
6/21	@ Minnesota	W 10-6	2nd	▼	1	Sox score seven runs in last three innings to avoid the sweep.
6/22	Seattle	W 14-10	2nd	▼	1	Martinez hits home run and drives in five.
6/23	Seattle	L 2-7	2nd	▼	1	Leake shuts out Sox over eight innings.
6/24	Seattle	W 5-0	1st	T		Sale dazzles with 13 Ks over seven innings.
6/26	Los Angeles Angels	W 9-1	2nd	▼	.5	Bradley Jr. goes 2-4 with a HR and four RBIs.
6/27	Los Angeles Angels	W 9-6	1st	▲	.5	Martinez hits league-leading 25th home run.
6/28	Los Angeles Angels	W 4-2	1st	▲	1	Sox sweep Angels season series (6-0) for first time in team history.
6/29	@ New York Yankees	L 1-8	1st	T		Sabathia shuts down Sox, Bird hits two homers.
6/30	@ New York Yankees	W 11-0	1st	▲	1	Devers goes 5-5 with grand slam; Sale allows 1 hit in 7 IP, fans 11.

JULY

DATE	OPPONENT	SCORE	PLACE			THE LOWDOWN
7/1	@ New York Yankees	L 1-11	1st	T		Hicks has three HR, Yankees pummel Price to tie division lead.
7/2	@ Washington	W 4-3	1st	▲	1	Rick Porcello hits three-run double off Scherzer.
7/3	@ Washington	W 11-4	1st	▲	1	Flurry of home runs powers Sox in blowout.
7/4	@ Washington	W 3-0	1st	▲	1	Rodriguez, 3 relievers allow 6 hits in shutout of Nationals.
7/6	@ Kansas City	W 10-5	1st	▲	2	Sale gives up one run over 6 IP (12 Ks).
7/7	@ Kansas City	W 15-4	1st	▲	2	Benintendi homers, doubles, and walks four times.
7/8	@ Kansas City	W 7-4	1st	▲	2	Kimbrel strikes out two for his 27th save of the season.
7/9	Texas	W 5-0	1st	▲	2.5	Pearce and Martinez homer, Sox win seventh in a row.
7/10	Texas	W 8-4	1st	▲	3.5	Benintendi hits two 2Bs, drives in 2.
7/11	Texas	W 4-2	1st	▲	3.5	Sale strikes out 12 for his 10th win of the year, Sox sweep.
7/12	Toronto	W 6-4	1st	▲	3.5	Betts hits grand slam in amazing 13-pitch at-bat.
7/13	Toronto	L 7-13	1st	▲	3.5	Pillar and Smoak combine for seven hits, 10-game win streak ends.
7/14	Toronto	W 6-2	1st	▲	3.5	Bogaerts hits walk-off grand slam in the 10th.
7/15	Toronto	W 5-2	1st	▲	4.5	All-Star break record best since 1949 (68-30).
7/20	@ Detroit	W 1-0	1st	▲	5.5	Pearce's RBI double enough to win as David Price stays sharp.
7/21	@ Detroit	L 0-5	1st	▲	4.5	Iglesias homers and drives in four.
7/22	@ Detroit	W 9-1	1st	▲	5	Sale dominance continues, strikes out 9 in six scoreless innings.
7/23	@ Baltimore	W 5-3	1st	▲	6	Porcello impresses again, Sox move 40 games above .500
7/24	@ Baltimore	L 6-7	1st	▲	5	Four Sox HRs not enough to take down O's.
7/26	Minnesota	L 1-2	1st	▲	4.5	Garver hits RBI double off Matt Barnes in the 8th.
7/27	Minnesota	W 4-3	1st	▲	5	Betts hits walk-off HR on the first pitch.
7/28	Minnesota	W 10-4	1st	▲	5.5	Martinez hits league-leading 32nd HR.
7/29	Minnesota	W 3-0	1st	▲	5.5	Eovaldi pitches seven scoreless innings in Sox debut.

DATE	OPPONENT	SCORE		PLACE		THE LOWDOWN
7/30	Philadelphia	W	2-1	1st	▲ 6	Holt's pinch-hit HR lifts Sox.
7/31	Philadelphia	L	1-3	1st	▲ 5	Sox hitters struggle vs. Jake Arrieta.

AUGUST

DATE	OPPONENT	SCORE		PLACE		THE LOWDOWN
8/2	New York Yankees	W	15-7	1st	▲ 6.5	Steven Pearce hits three home runs.
8/3	New York Yankees	W	4-1	1st	▲ 7.5	Cora ejected, Porcello pitches 1-hitter.
8/4	New York Yankees	W	4-1	1st	▲ 8.5	Eovaldi pitches eight scoreless innings.
8/5	New York Yankees	W	5-4	1st	▲ 9.5	Sox complete 4-game sweep in walkoff.
8/7	@ Toronto	W	10-7	1st	▲ 9	Kimbrel blows the save but five runs in the 10th win it for Sox.
8/8	@ Toronto	W	10-5	1st	▲ 9	Devers hits HR in first game back from DL.
8/9	@ Toronto	L	5-8	1st	▲ 8	Betts hits for his first career cycle.
8/10	@ Baltimore	W	19-12	1st	▲ 9	Bogaerts and Benintendi each hit three HRs.
8/11	@ Baltimore	W	5-0	1st	▲ 9.5	Price fans 10, Bradley Jr. hits two HRs.
8/11	@ Baltimore	W	6-4	1st	▲ 9.5	Martinez hits go-ahead HR in the 8th (his second of the day).
8/12	@ Baltimore	W	4-1	1st	▲ 9.5	Sale returns from DL, outduels Alex Cobb.
8/14	@ Philadelphia	W	2-1	1st	▲ 10	Holt blasts pinch-hit HR, Sox take 10-game lead in AL East.
8/15	@ Philadelphia	L	4-7	1st	▲ 10	Ramos has three hits in Phillies debut.
8/17	Tampa Bay	W	7-3	1st	▲ 10.5	Sox pitch eight scoreless innings after allowing three runs in the first.
8/18	Tampa Bay	W	5-2	1st	▲ 10.5	Martinez hits league-leading 38th HR.
8/19	Tampa Bay	L	0-2	1st	▲ 9.5	Beeks blanks Sox a month after they traded him.
8/20	Cleveland	L	4-5	1st	▲ 9	Allen hits go-ahead HR after Porcello leaves with injury.
8/21	Cleveland	L	3-6	1st	▲ 8	Bieber outpitches Eovaldi in his Major League debut.
8/22	Cleveland	W	10-4	1st	▲ 9	Bogaerts hits two homers.
8/23	Cleveland	W	7-0	1st	▲ 9.5	Price (8 IP, 0 ER, 7 K) wins fifth start in a row.
8/24	@ Tampa Bay	L	3-10	1st	▲ 8.5	Beeks earns second win over his former team.
8/25	@ Tampa Bay	L	1-5	1st	▲ 7	Sox bats stagnant as Rays win seventh straight.
8/26	@ Tampa Bay	L	1-9	1st	▲ 6	Snell Ks eight as Sox get swept for first time all season.
8/28	Miami	W	8-7	1st	▲ 6.5	JT Riddle has costly error in the 9th.
8/29	Miami	W	14-6	1st	▲ 7.5	Sox score 11 runs in the 7th.
8/30	@ Chicago White Sox	W	9-4	1st	▲ 8.5	Sox break the tie with five runs in the 9th.
8/31	@ Chicago White Sox	L	1-6	1st	▲ 7.5	Moncada homers off Eovaldi.

SEPTEMBER

DATE	OPPONENT	SCORE		PLACE		THE LOWDOWN
9/1	@ Chicago White Sox	W	6-1	1st	▲ 7.5	Rodriguez strikes out 12 in 5 2/3 innings.
9/2	@ Chicago White Sox	L	0-8	1st	▲ 7.5	Shields, Anderson, and Palka combine for the shutout.
9/3	@ Atlanta	W	8-2	1st	▲ 8.5	Sox score five runs in final two innings.
9/4	@ Atlanta	W	5-1	1st	▲ 8.5	Pearce impresses again with three hits, three RBI.
9/5	@ Atlanta	W	9-8	1st	▲ 9.5	Phillips' winning HR in season debut caps rally from 7-1 deficit.
9/7	Houston	L	3-6	1st	▲ 8.5	Sox bullpen loses two-run lead, gives up 6.
9/8	Houston	L	3-5	1st	▲ 7.5	Bregman hits a homer, Rodriguez gives up 5 ER.
9/9	Houston	W	6-5	1st	▲ 8.5	Moreland hits walk-off single.
9/11	Toronto	W	7-2	1st	▲ 9	Holt homers, Sox become first team in MLB to clinch playoff spot.
9/12	Toronto	W	1-0	1st	▲ 10	Price dazzles again, Sox reach 100 wins.
9/13	Toronto	W	4-3	1st	▲ 10.5	Martinez hits 41st HR of the season, Sox sweep.
9/14	New York Mets	L	0-8	1st	▲ 9.5	Sox can't get to Syndergaard (7 IP, 6 Ks).
9/15	New York Mets	W	5-3	1st	▲ 10.5	Holt pinch-hits and gets tie-breaking double.
9/16	New York Mets	W	4-3	1st	▲ 11.5	Sox score three runs off deGrom.
9/18	@ New York Yankees	L	2-3	1st	▲ 10.5	Walker hits three-run HR.
9/19	@ New York Yankees	L	1-10	1st	▲ 9.5	Voit homers twice off David Price.
9/20	@ New York Yankees	W	11-6	1st	▲ 10.5	Betts 4-5 with 5 RBIs as Sox clinch AL East title.
9/21	@ Cleveland	W	7-5	1st	▲ 10.5	Sam Travis and Tzu-Wei Lin hit first career HRs.
9/22	@ Cleveland	L	4-5	1st	▲ 9.5	Brantley hits walk-off single in the 11th.
9/23	@ Cleveland	L	3-4	1st	▲ 9.5	Allen hits walk-off single in the 11th.
9/24	Baltimore	W	6-2	1st	▲ 9.5	Sox break franchise record with 106th win of the season.
9/26	Baltimore	W	19-3	1st	▲ 9.5	Sox hand O's a franchise-record 112th loss of the season.
9/26	Baltimore	L	3-10	1st	▲ 9.5	Sox bullpen gives up seven runs.
9/28	New York Yankees	L	6-11	1st	▲ 8	Yanks clinch wild-card home field.
9/29	New York Yankees	L	5-8	1st	▲ 7	Yankees break MLB home run record, earn 100th win.
9/30	New York Yankees	W	10-2	1st	▲ 8	Sox win 108th game, Betts clinches batting title.

Mookie Betts
OUTFIELDER

J.D. Martinez
DH/OUTFIELDER

LED THE MAJORS with 10.9 WAR.

LED THE MAJORS with a .346 average and .640 slugging pct.

RANKED 2ND IN MLB IN OBP (.438), OPS (1.078), and extra-base hits (84).

FIRST RED SOX PLAYER to win the AL batting title since Bill Mueller in 2003 and the first to lead the majors since Wade Boggs, below, in 1988.

SECOND RED SOX HITTER ever with 30+ HR and 30+ SB in the same season (Jacoby Ellsbury, 2011).

.346 .330
AVERAGE

32 43
HOME RUNS

80 130
RUNS BATTED IN

.438 .402
ON-BASE PERCENTAGE

.640 .629
SLUGGING PERCENTAGE

LED MLB WITH 130 RBIS and 358 total bases.

WAS 2ND IN MLB with .330 batting average and 43 HRs.

BECAME THIRD RED SOX ever to hit at least .330 with 40+ HR and 130+ RBIs, joining Ted Williams, below (1949), and Jimmie Foxx (1936, '38).

HIS 43 HRS were a Red Sox record in a player's first season with the club.

THE RED SOX WENT 35-5 when he homered and 60-10 when he drove in at least 1 run.

BY CHAD FINN • Globe Staff

Ain't no stopping us now

Good times never seemed so good? Got that right, Neil Diamond. And here's the best news for Boston sports fans: The good times are poised to last.

The Red Sox have now won their fourth World Series since 2004, when they swept the St. Louis Cardinals to exorcise all ghosts and lift all curses and then went on to win in '07 and '13. The change in centuries has worked out quite well for them.

But this latest trophy enhances an even more impressive tale: the staggering 21st century success of Boston professional sports, and the youthful rosters on at least three of the teams that promise more championships, more duck boats, for years to come.

Since the 2001 Patriots ended a 15-year title drought in Boston sports by stunning the St. Louis Rams (a 14-point favorite in Las Vegas), 20-17, in Super Bowl XXXVI, this city hasn't just been the home of champions. It's been the home of contender after contender after contender, from the Patriots to the Red Sox to the Celtics and Bruins, across all seasons, for practically a full generation of fans.

Beginning with the 2001 Patriots, there have been 67 separate seasons among the Patriots, Red Sox, Celtics, and Bruins. (The 2004-05 Bruins season was lost to an NHL lockout.) In that time, 51 teams have made the playoffs, 39 have reached the final eight teams playing, 26 have reached the final four and 16, with the Red Sox being the latest, have made the championship round.

The 2018 Red Sox are the 11th Boston team to win a championship in 18 years. The Patriots have won five in eight visits to the Super Bowl. The Celtics and Bruins each have made the Finals twice in that span, coming away with a championship one title apiece.

Know what qualifies as the bad old days during this sports century? The seasons 2005-06, the only consecutive years that Boston — gasp! — didn't have at least one team reach its sport's final round. The Celtics have the longest championship drought among the four teams at 10 years, having last won in 2008 (they lost in seven games to the Lakers in 2010).

Much to the annoyance of the rest of the sports world, Boston teams remain positioned to contend for years to come. Perhaps the window could close soon on the Patriots, the greatest prolonged dynasty in the history of the NFL, with five Super Bowl wins in the Bill Belichick/Tom Brady era. After all, Belichick is now 66 and Brady is 41. But the Patriots do have young talent on the roster and coaching staff, including offensive coordinator Josh McDaniels, who is 42.

There is no doubt the Patriots have created the blueprint that the other Boston franchises follow, beginning in 2001: draft and retain the best of a home-grown core, surround young talent with bright, innovative and communicative coaches, mix in the right accomplished players via free agency and trades, tweak the recipe here and there, then be ready to handle success, because it's going to come.

Belichick is a legend in his own time, but the other coaches on Boston's scene are making their own names. Brad Stevens took the Celtics to Game 7 of the Eastern Conference finals last year despite the absence of Gordon Hayward and Kyrie Irving, arguably his two best players. Bruce Cassidy led the Bruins to a 50-20-12 record in his first full year on the job. And Alex Cora led the Red Sox to a franchise-record 108 regular season wins and a World Series in his first year as a manager.

Other fanbases aren't going to care to hear this, but the greatest evidence that these good old days can last even longer is the caliber of young talent across the rosters right now. Celtics budding star Jayson Tatum is just 20. Bruins defenseman Charlie McAvoy is 20, Brandon Carlo is 21, and there are several blossoming 22-year-olds, among them David Pastrnak, Jake DeBrusk, and Ryan Donato. The Celtics' Jaylen Brown and Red Sox third baseman Rafael Devers both turned 22 on Oct. 24, and Red Sox outfielder Andrew Benintendi is 24.

As for Mookie Betts and Xander Bogaerts, well, their joints must crackle and creak when they get out of bed. They both turned 26 in October, the same age as Irving.

In the final episode of the television show "The Office," the character Andy Bernard, played by Ed Helms, had a memorable line: "I wish," he said, "that there was a way to know you were in the good old days before you actually left them."

Boston's sports teams have been living in the good old days for more than a decade. We know we're in them, and one never can be sure, but we also think we know this: They don't look like they're going to end anytime soon. ■

"A.C. has set the right tone. He believes in us and we believe in him."

MOOKIE BETTS